Money Management For Teens: Financial Literacy and Practical Skills for Financial Independence, Even for Those Who Don't Come From Money

Robert E. Baines, Jr., D.Min.

Thank You

As my way of saying "thank you" for purchasing my book,
go to https://bit.ly/25WaysTeensFI
for a free copy of my

"25 Ways Parents and Caregivers Can Help Their Teenagers Become Financially Independent by Their 40th Birthday (Or Sooner)."

Money Management For Teens: Financial Literacy and Practical Skills for Financial Independence, Even for Those Who Don't Come From Money

Copyright © 2024 by Robert E. Baines, Jr.

Published by RDA Solutions LLC

ISBN: 9798338618233

RDA Solutions LLC
2915 Timbercrest Drive, Suite 204
Cincinnati, Ohio 45238

Printed in the United States of America
First Edition

Disclaimer: The information in this book, Money Management for Teens, is intended for educational and informational purposes only. It is not financial, legal, or professional advice, and should not be construed as such. The author, Robert E. Baines, Jr., is not a licensed financial advisor, and the information presented herein may not be suitable for your specific situation.

Acknowledgements and Dedication

Anytime you do something worthwhile, it is normally a team effort. My team includes God who has given me the desire, skills, time freedom, and resources to write another book. I'm thankful for my wife, Daphene Baines, for her continued support in all that I do. I'm thankful to the A.I. Publishing Academy for helping me develop this book and get it published. I'm thankful for my father who did a good job of inspiring me to use my gifts to be a blessing to others.

I dedicate this book to my grandchildren who were only 5 (Caleb), 8 (LilyGrace), and 10 (Jared) years old at the time of this writing. I dedicate this book teenagers through out the United States and the world. I pray that you will be the first or next financially independent person in your family and community. I further pray that you use your resources to be a blessing to others.

A Word to Parents and Caregivers

Despite the United States being one of the richest nations in the world, way too many people are working 40 years of their lives and still ending up in poverty or uncomfortably close to it. Some people reach their 70s without having ever made much money; therefore, they have no wealth. Others made good money but spent it all, so they have no wealth. In 2024, very few people can count on a pension from their job, and social security is a question mark for the next generation.

If you want your teenagers to have a fighting chance at making a great income and becoming financially independent, you must get this book for them! I will walk them through the following:

- The importance of having a "money mindset" as well as how to develop one
- Making decisions about focusing on money or school as a teenager
- Earning high after high school. This chapter includes practical discussion about how college fits or doesn't fit into their future.
- Spending low
- Investing wisely, yes, even as a teenager
- Four case studies to allow some practical reflection
- How to build their customized action plan for financial independence

This book started as my desire to ensure that my young grandchildren had a guide for managing their money. But it has grown to be a guide that teenagers around the country and perhaps the world can use for the same purpose.

I'm thankful that by the grace of God, my wife and I did pretty well for ourselves. But I earnestly pray for the generations that are coming behind us. Even though young people are much more familiar with using technology than my peers, I don't see the school, church, or family teaching them about financial literacy or financial discipline. **Do your young people a favor and purchase this book for them!**

Table of Contents

Introduction

Fifteen-year-old Marcus had a decision to make. Would he spend the $150 that he worked for two weeks to get on a pair of all-white Air Force 1s to add to his collection, or would he save the money for the car that he wants to purchase after he graduates from high school? This moment, a battle between short-term instant gratification and longer-term goals, is one many teens face, often without the right tools to make informed decisions.

This book is born from a simple but powerful belief: *with the proper knowledge and skills, financial independence is within reach for almost all teens in advanced countries (e.g., United States, Canada, Australia, United Kingdom, etc.), no matter their background.* It is designed to be more than just a guide. It is a roadmap to developing a "money mindset," earning high, spending low, and investing wisely. Through practical discussions, helpful exercises, and personal reflection questions, this book will guide you in crafting your customized action plan for financial independence.

"I'm Just a Teenager" ... Who is This Book For?

As a teen, you might wonder how a book about finances could be of interest. You might think, "I'm too young to worry about money," or "I'll deal with finances later." But here's the truth: the sooner you understand and manage your money, the sooner you can be financially independent.

You cannot count on getting a job with a company, working 40 years, and living off of a nice pension. Nor can you count on working job after job for 40 years and then living off of social security. **If you want to kick back and enjoy living your life without having to go to work, you need to learn about and start working towards financial independence as soon as possible.**

This book includes diverse stories and examples, particularly resonating with African American teens, those from working-class families, and those from single-parent households.

Why Should You Listen to Me?

My grandfather was a sharecropper in the South, before migrating with his family to the North to do manual labor with less than a third grade education. My father was born in the South and picked cotton, until he migrated with his family to the North. But he was able to apply himself and become a journeyman electrician and then a prominent Baptist Pastor. On one hand, I have experienced what it means to be on welfare with food stamps. I have had to piece together financial aid and take one or two courses at a time, while working full-time with a young family. But on the other hand, I have had the privilege to earn advanced degrees (e.g., Doctor of Ministry degree with a focus on economic and spiritual empowerment) and accumulate enough wealth for my wife and me to live comfortably. This book is written from the perspective of a grandfather who deeply cares about the financial independence of future generations.

How is This Book Structured?

The following chapters cover *the four pillars of financial independence – having a "money mindset," earning high, spending low, and investing wisely.* Each chapter contains "good to know" information, practical exercises, and reflection questions that help you develop your customized action plan for financial independence.

In Chapter 1, we will look at some sad financial numbers in the United States and your ability to become financially independent despite those numbers. We will define "money mindset," talk about why it is important to have it, and how to develop and maintain it. *Without the right mindset, you will not be able to consistently do what you need to do to be financially independent.*

In Chapter 2, we will discuss the question of "Should teenagers focus on making money, going to school, or both"? There is no one size fits all. I will share practical tips for those who focus on school only, money only, or both.

In Chapter 3, we will discuss "earning high." We will cover the importance of understanding your aptitudes, financial outlooks, and demand. *We will discuss how college is for some people but not everyone.*

In Chapter 4, we will discuss "spending low." We will talk about how your money personality, emotions, and peers can impact your spending habits. I will give you some practical tips on how to get more value for less money. I will also give you some *useful tips regarding buying your first car, getting your first apartment, and paying for college.*

In Chapter 5, we will discuss "investing wisely." We will discuss the difference between saving and investing. You need savings for things like your emergency fund and large purchases. But you must have investments that can outperform the drag of inflation. We will look at 7 ways to invest your money. *We will even discuss how to start with $5 and pocket change.*

In Chapter 6, we will discuss four case studies. Each study features a teenager who made some decisions, took some actions, and experienced some realities. This chapter will really help you think through where you want to be after high school and expose you to different paths to financial independence.

In Chapter 7, we will work through a process to help you develop your customized action plan for YOUR FINANCIAL INDEPENDENCE. We will discuss your WHY, inspiration, SMART goals, account-ability, and the need for consistent strategic action in the four areas/pillars of financial independence.

How Can You Get the Most Out of This Book?

I recommend you read this entire book, with a friend or two, to familiarize yourself with the concepts. Then, revisit each chapter to complete the review and reflection questions. Most importantly, develop a customized action plan to achieve your financial independence.

No matter what you have been through or are going through, let this be the beginning of your journey towards financial independence. Embrace this challenge with an open mind and determination. The knowledge and skills you are about to acquire will not only benefit you. You will be able to share them with others in your family and community.

So, let's get started. Turn the page and enter a world where financial independence isn't just a dream—it's your achievable future.

Chapter 1. Money Mindset

As Sarah, a 16-year-old high school student, stared at her dwindling bank balance on her mobile app, she felt the increase weight of upcoming college expenses and the desire for a new laptop for school. Her part-time job at the local fast food restaurant seemed barely enough, and with each swipe of her card, her anxiety about the future grew. She was losing confidence in her ability to do any better than her working class parents and grandparents who lived paycheck to paycheck.

In this chapter, we will discuss some sad numbers about how so many people work all of their working lives to simply live in poverty. We will then quickly talk about how YOU can become financially independent, if you are willing to work on your "money mindset" and the other three pillars of financial independence (i.e., earn high, spend low, and invest wisely).

Some Sad Numbers ...

In the United States, a staggering number of individuals live paycheck to paycheck, with little to no savings, only to retire into poverty. Recent statistics reveal a grim picture: according to Forbes,[i] approximately 78% of United States workers live paycheck to paycheck. This isn't just confined to low-income earners. Nearly 10% of workers earning $100,000 or more also report that they usually or always live paycheck to paycheck.[ii] As of 2022, according to the US Census, the average per capita income (i.e., the average of what each person earns) in the United States was $37,683.[iii]

On top of these sad numbers, the median retirement savings for ages 65-74 is only about $200,000.[iv] According to the Social Security Administration, the average Social Security check amounts to about $1,907 per month ($22,884/yr.),[v] which is barely enough to cover basic living expenses, let alone provide a comfortable retirement. At 67, when many aspire to retire, the average American has nowhere near enough saved or invested to sustain their pre-retirement standard of living even with their expected Social Security income.

Think about becoming too old to work to make money, not having enough money saved or invested, not having enough coming in from the government, and not having anything coming in from a company pension, but you still have living expenses like food, housing, and medicine. Think about working 40 years and when it is time to retire, you have your income cut from $37,683/year (see average per capita above) to $22,884/year (see Social Security above) and hoping that you don't outlive the money you have saved and invested for retirement. This is what tens of millions of Americans are facing.

This financial insecurity stems significantly from a "gap in financial education." Most elementary and high schools offer enough teaching in mathematics, science, and literature but fall significantly short in practical financial education. Family and faith communities cannot be counted on to teach financial literacy or financial discipline. The consequences of this "gap in financial education" are not minor. There are generations of adults who find themselves unprepared for the financial realities of adulthood, retirement, and everything in between.

Yet, Financial Independence is Possible for YOU!!!

Financial independence occurs when the cash flow from your investments covers all your living expenses. Imagine not having to work unless you choose to because the income from your investments - be it real estate, stocks, or other assets - covers everything from your housing to your food and leisure activities. For instance, if your yearly expenses total $75,000, achieving financial independence means you have at least $75,000/year coming to you from your investments.

Here are three great reasons to become financially independence as soon as possible:

1. *Comfort.* It affords you a comfortable living where every day financial pressures like rent, groceries, utilities, and car maintenance are easily managed without having to go to a job.

2. *Travel.* It provides the freedom to travel. Imagine having the money and time flexibility to explore Africa, Europe, and South America. You could also take road trips across the United States and relax on Caribbean beaches, while others are tied to their jobs.

3. *Help Others.* Financial independence allows you to support causes you believe in, whether helping family members in need, donating to churches and charities, or investing in community projects.

It may be difficult for you to see right now, but no matter your family background, you can learn the lessons in this book. You can implement this material and become the first or next financially independent person in your family and community. Think about how you will feel when you have enough income coming in from your investments to live comfortably, travel as you would like, and be able to help whoever you would like. Think about how you will feel when you inspire and help others do the same.

Alex and Jamie
Consider two teens: Alex and Jamie. Both were students in public high schools, lived in single parent working class families, and had no mentoring in becoming financial independent. Alex was given this book as a teenager and applied its principles diligently. By age 32, he had achieved financial independence, with investments yielding enough annual income to cover all his personal expenses and then some.

Jamie, on the other hand, was given the same book as a teenager. But he didn't even read it. He believed he would be like all the working class people in his life. He saw himself as a victim of his upbringing. By the age of 32, he found himself in a job he hated, living paycheck to paycheck, and had no plan to improve his situation anytime soon.

What is the difference between these two? One studied this book and took consistent strategic action to achieve financial independence. The other just gave in to the negativity of his surroundings. *Do you want to be more like Alex or Jamie?*

The impact of starting early on your financial journey cannot be overstated. If, for example, you begin investing $500 a month at a 10% annual return starting at age 20, by the time you reach age 50, you could be looking at an account balance of over $1,000,000. Delaying this start until age 40 dramatically reduces your potential, yielding about $100,000 by age 50 under the same conditions. The 20 year delay will cost you $900,000.

Increasing your monthly investment to $1,000 can accelerate your progress, reaching $1,000,000 around age 43.[vi] The principle here is clear: the earlier you start, the quicker you can reach financial independence.

Achieving such independence rests on four pillars: having a "money mindset," earning high, spending low, and investing wisely. This book can help you understand concepts and take the actions you need to take toward your financial independence and help others do the same.

"Money Mindset"

Henry Ford famously said, "Whether you think you can, or you think you can't — you're right." This simple yet profound adage underscores the pivotal role of mindset in shaping your life. As a teenager stepping into financial management, embracing the right mindset will be of foundational importance to you. The mountains of financial challenges and societal pressures can seem impossible, but with a "money mindset," you can succeed anyhow.

Let's define 'money mindset' more concretely. **"Money mindset" is having a practical understanding of financial independence (knowledge), a realistic action plan (plan), and the determination to execute this plan despite obstacles (grit).** So, you need to learn the concepts and practices involved in financial independence. This includes continuing education, since the landscape of money management is ever evolving. You need to develop and update your action plan as needed. There are different paths. You need to plan YOUR path to financial independence. And you must build

21

and maintain your grit – mental toughness – to work around and through challenges.

How to Develop and Maintain a "Money Mindset"

Even if no one is supporting you, you can have a "money mindset." Developing and maintaining a strong "money mindset" involves the following 6 strategic steps:

1. Believe. Believe that you can become financially independent. "The journey of a thousand miles begins with one step," Lao Tzu. Becoming financially independent will not be easy or quick. But if you keep working towards it and walking in the right direction, you can get there. If you don't believe this, you are right; you will not do it. If you have enough belief to keep doing the work, you may get there quicker than you think. Some people have started with much less than you have and made it. Make up your mind that you are going to make this journey.

You may lack self-confidence. But here are three great ways to increase your level of belief that you can do this:

1. Study the Following Stories:
- Moziah Bridges. He started his own bow tie business, Mo's Bows, at the age of 9. He learned how to sew from his grandmother and began making bow ties that quickly gained popularity. He faced challenges in managing the business as a young entrepreneur and balancing it with schoolwork. By the age of 15, Moziah had made significant profits and even secured a licensing deal with the NBA.[vii]

- Leanna Archer. She began her own hair care product line, Leanna's Inc., when she was just 9 years old, using her grandmother's secret recipes. She had to overcome skepticism due to her age and manage the complexities of running a business as a student. By her teenage years, Leanna's business had grown significantly, earning over $100,000 in annual revenue.[viii]

- Fraser Doherty. He started making jams from his grandmother's recipes at the age of 14 and began selling them to neighbors and local shops. He had to refine his product and business model. He faced competition and the difficulties of scaling production. By the age of 16, Fraser's company, SuperJam, was supplying major United Kingdom supermarkets, and he became a millionaire in his teens.[ix]

- Catherine Cook. She and her brother co-founded MyYearbook.com at the age of 15. The idea was to create a social networking site for high school students. They faced the challenge of developing and marketing a new social media platform in a competitive space. MyYearbook grew rapidly and was later sold for $100 million, making Catherine financially independent in her late teens.[x]

- Nick D'Aloisio. He developed the mobile app Summly at the age of 15, which condensed news articles into summaries. He encountered difficulties in coding, funding, and gaining recognition for his app as a young developer. Yahoo acquired Summly for approximately $30 million when Nick was just 17, securing his financial independence.[xi]

2. *Search* "how to build my confidence as a teenager" and study articles like "Confidence and Self-Esteem – for 11-18 Year Olds"[xii]

3. Find a Mentor. Having a trusted adult provide guidance and answer questions can boost your confidence. Mentors can share their experiences and successes, making financial independence seem more attainable.

2. Learn. This book will give you a great start in your financial literacy. However, there are other topics you need to study or study in more detail as you travel towards your financial independence. Some resources will be easy to study, and some will be boring. When you need to study something boring, studying in 10-minute periods may help you keep going (i.e., a few steps in the right direction). Make sure you look at the resources listed in the back of this book.

Search "great books for teenagers to read to increase their financial literacy." The following are three great books for you to start ready:
- **Rich Dad, Poor Dad for Teens** by Robert T. Kiyosaki
- **Think and Grow Rich: A Black Choice** by Dennis Kimbro and Napoleon Hill
- **I Will Teach You to Be Rich** by Ramit Sethi

3. Plan. This book will guide you through the process of developing your action plan for financial independence. Having goals, plans, inspiration, and accountability are crucial. No matter how well thought out your plan may be, you can expect to make some tweaks and revisions as you go. That is fine. When you have an action plan, at least you have something to revise. Most people don't even have a plan to revise.

Commit to working through this book, which has a chapter on developing an action plan for your financial independence. Search "How to make an action plan for financial independence as a teenager."

4. Work. Believing, understanding information, and having a plan mean nothing, if you don't take action. Because the journey to financial independence can be so long, tracking your actions is to your advantage. We will talk about daily, weekly, and monthly actions aimed at your financial independence later in the book. But for now, understand that tracking your actions will give you a sense of accomplishment (i.e., some instant gratification) along the way, instead of just waiting until you reach the big goal of being financially independent.

5. Your Support System. You need to have a plan to have and keep some people around you who will help you keep working towards your financial independence as they work on theirs. And you need to have a plan to keep negative influences from distracting you from being consistent in your financial independence work.

Study the article *"How To Build and Maintain a Strong Support System for Teenagers."*[xiii] Search "tips for teenagers trying to build a positive support system."

6. Keep Your Mind Right, Despite Challenges. Journaling and daily reviewing your action plan (see later chapter), which includes your WHY and inspirational material will be helpful in this area. Make a daily journal note about how you are coming with carrying out your action plan. Study the article *"10 Health and Well-being Perks of Journaling for Teenagers."*[xiv] Search "How to be more consistent in carrying out my action plan for financial independence as a teenager." Search "Tips for teenagers to stay focused and disciplined, despite challenges in their lives."

Work through questions like the following when you run into challenges:

- What happened?
- How do I feel about what happened?
- What thoughts support these feelings?
- How do these feelings relate to my carrying out my financial independence plan?
- How do I want to feel?
- What do I need to focus on to feel how I want to feel?
- What do I need to do to get back on track or to stay on track?
- What advice would I give someone going through a similar situation?

This exercise will help you get back on track with carrying out your action plan, instead of being distracted by unhelpful feelings and thoughts.

So, there you have it. Six steps to developing and maintaining a "money mindset." Start with believing that **you can do this**. Keep learning as you plan your work and work your plan. Develop your support system and keep your mind right, especially when facing challenges.

Watch the Company That YOU Keep

Peer pressure is a potent force in the lives of teenagers, often shaping their spending behaviors and decisions more than they might realize. This is not merely about choosing which movie to see or what clothes to wear. It extends to how well you stay consistent in carrying out your action plan for financial independence.

Jim Rohn famously said, "You're the average of the five people you spend the most time with." Think about how this relates to your financial independence. If you are consistently around peers who waste money and are not trying to get ahead, it will often have a negative pull on your being consistent with carrying out your action plan. Thankfully, if you are always around peers who are reading about financial literacy and personal development and who practice wise spending habits, it will often have a positive push with your being consistent with carrying out your action plan. Not only should you be thinking about your family and friends, but think about who you claim to be your boyfriend or girlfriend.

The following are some practical tips for dealing with peer pressure:

1. Negative Influences. When someone is influencing you to abandon your action plan, you need to work on saying "no" to their influence. At some point, you need to ask, "Why are you interacting so much with them"? The answer may be that they are family. They may be good friends in other areas. They may be co-workers with whom you have to get along. If you have to interact with them or choose to interact with them, work on discussing things you all agree on instead of financial matters. If you don't have to interact with them, you may want to limit or eliminate interacting with them.

2. Positive Influences. When you have someone who is influencing you to be consistent in carrying out your action plan, work on interacting with them regularly. You may find this type of person among your family members and friends, at school, at a financial independence club, at your place of worship, etc. A great way to attract this kind of person is to be this kind of person (i.e., positive influence with a money mindset). Ask responsible adults for any help they can render. *Think about finding or developing a group of teens who study this book together, sharing their answers to the review and reflection questions, and serving as an accountability group for one another (see appendix for some tips).*

As We Close This Chapter ...

In this chapter, we have discussed the following material:
- The overwhelming majority of Americans will work for many years and yet get nowhere near financial independence.
- YOU have the opportunity and ability to learn from this book and start taking action towards your financial independence.
- YOU have enough information to start working on your "money mindset" – believe, learn, plan, and work while developing your support system and keeping your mind right, especially as you deal with challenges.
- YOU must manage negative peer pressure and nurture positive peer pressure.

So, we talked about having a "money mindset." But what about making some money right now? The next chapter will discuss "making money as a teenager." But before we do, let's work through the following review and reflection questions:

Review Questions:
1. A. Based on this chapter, what percentage of Americans live paycheck to paycheck?

B. What is the average per capita income?

C. At what age do most people hope to retire, and what is the median amount saved by this age?

D. How much is the average monthly Social Security check?

2. A. Financial independence occurs when the cash flow generated from your i _____ is sufficient to cover

living e_____.

B. Three benefits of being financially independent are: 1. Able to live c _____, 2. Able to t _____, and 3. Able to h_____ others.

C. If a person invested $500/month from age 20 to age 50 at 10% return/year, they would have about _____. If they invested $1,000/month from age 20 to age 43 at 10% return/year, they would have about _____. But if they wait until age 40 to start investing $500/month until age 50 at 10%/year, they will only have about _____.

D. We will cover four pillars of financial independence in this book: 1. Having a "_____ mindset," 2. _____ high, 3. _____ low, and 4. _____ wisely.

3. A. A "Money mindset" is having a practical understanding of f _____ independence (knowledge), a realistic a _____ plan (plan), and the determination to e _____ this plan despite obstacles (grit).

B. The six steps for developing and maintaining a "money mindset" are 1. B____, 2. L _____, 3. P _____, and 4. W _____, while 5. developing your s _____ s _____ and 6. keeping your m_____ right, especially as you deal with c_____.

4. A. According to Jim Rohn, "You're the average of the f_____ p_____ you spend the most time with."

B. With negative influences, you have to l_____ or e _____ interacting with some people. With positive influences, you have to

29

nurture relationships with these people by being a p_____ influence in the lives of others.

Reflection Questions

1. Think about how you will feel if you worked until age 67 and had to keep working because you didn't have enough money to retire. Now, think about the comfort, travel, and ability to help people that can come with financial independence. Would you rather be working hard at age 67 with no real relief in sight or be financially independent by the age of 40? Explain.

2. Henry Ford famously said, "Whether you think you can or you think you can't — you're right." Do you believe that you can study this book and start taking steps towards your financial independence? Explain.

3. As you think through the six steps for developing and maintaining a money mindset, list two or three things next to each step that you can do to help you build and maintain your money mindset.
Believe -
Learn -
Plan -
Work -
Support -
Keep your mind right -
Your responses will help you develop your action plan in the later chapter.

4. List the 10 people you spend the most time with. On a scale of one to five, with five being high, how would you grade there being a positive influence? Given their grade, what should you do? Do you have enough 4s and 5s? If not, how will you get them?

Chapter 2. As a Teenager, "Should You Focus on Making Money or Going to School"?

Imagine a teenager, let's call her Emma, standing at the crossroads of a decision that could shape her financial future. She has just been offered a part-time job at a local bookstore, a dream for any avid reader. However, accepting the job would mean less time for her studies and extracurricular activities, which are vital for her college applications. Emma's dilemma is not unique. It is a situation that many teens face. The decision to focus on earning money or concentrating solely on schoolwork can be difficult and significantly impact your path to financial independence.

Remember from Chapter 1 that the four pillars of financial independence are: 1. Having a "money mindset," 2. Earning high, 3. Spending low, and 4. Investing wisely. In the last chapter, we discussed having a "money mindset." In this chapter, we will discuss issues related to focusing on making money or your education as a teenager.

Decisions, Decisions, Decisions

Whether to prioritize making money over schooling, or vice versa, is complex and depends on individual circumstances, goals, and the current economic environment. For some teens like Emma, entering the workforce is compelling and necessary, perhaps due to financial constraints at home or the desire to start saving for major expenses like a training program, college tuition, or a car. On the other hand, focusing solely on academics can lead to better long-term career opportunities, potentially resulting in higher earnings.

What is the Big Deal About Going to College?

The following are some of the biggest reasons people focus on going to college:

- *Higher Earning Potential.* College graduates often earn significantly more over their lifetimes compared to those with only a high school diploma. A degree can open doors to higher-paying job opportunities and career advancements.
- *Broader Career Opportunities.* Many professions require a college degree as a minimum qualification. Fields such as medicine, engineering, law, and academia typically require advanced education.
- *Personal Growth and Development.* College offers an environment for personal growth, including critical thinking, problem-solving, and communication skills. The college experience can help teenagers develop independence, self-discipline, and a sense of responsibility.
- *Networking Opportunities.* College provides numerous opportunities to build a professional network. Connections made with peers, professors, and industry professionals can be valuable for future career prospects.
- *Access to Resources and Support.* Colleges offer various resources, including libraries, labs, career services, and counseling. These resources can support academic and professional success.

The following are some of the biggest reasons people may **not** focus on going to college:

- *High Cost and Debt.* The cost of college tuition, fees, and living expenses can lead to significant student loan debt. Many students graduate with substantial debt, which can be a financial burden for years.

- *Time Commitment.* Earning a degree typically takes at least four years of full-time study. This time commitment may delay entry into the workforce and the start of earning a full-time income.
- *Uncertain Job Market.* A college degree does not guarantee a job, and some graduates may struggle to find employment in their field. The job market can be competitive, and graduates might face underemployment or jobs unrelated to their major.
- *Opportunity Cost.* Time spent in college could be spent gaining work experience or starting a business. Some teenagers might find more success and satisfaction by pursuing alternative paths to financial independence.
- *Stress and Pressure.* The academic and social pressures of college can be overwhelming for some students. Balancing coursework, exams, and personal life can lead to stress, anxiety, and burnout.

Think about how it is possible to be a college graduate with a good job or profitable business but not be happy or financially independent. Consider how you can become financially independent without a college degree and always go to college after you are financially independent for the sake of enrichment courses.

There is no one-size-fits-all. College is great for some people. And college is a big distraction for others. As a teenager, you need to decide how college fits or does not fit into your plans for financial independence. If you had to choose, are you trying to have a college degree or be financially independent?

Focusing on Making Money

For teenagers who lean towards earning over schooling, the immediate benefit is making money. This income can support family finances, save for future expenses, or fund personal projects. Moreover, working part-time can teach valuable life skills such as time management, responsibility, customer service, and the value of hard work. These experiences provide practical knowledge that is not always taught in classrooms.

However, there are downsides. The most significant is the potential impact on educational outcomes. Balancing job hours with schoolwork can be challenging. There is a risk that your academic performance could decline, which might affect college admissions and future career prospects. Furthermore, focusing predominantly on work might limit exposure to other significant developmental experiences during teenage years, such a leadership opportunities, sports, or creative pursuits, which are also valuable in personal growth and college applications.

Just for the sake of covering all the bases, *"all money is not good money."* Some teenagers think about making money in illegal ways like selling drugs, prostitution, stealing, or robbing. First, many people who try to make money in these ways never make the money. Many end up in prison, hurt, or dead. Second, even if you make the money, how will you feel about yourself? You don't want to make money and then feel terrible about yourself. Third, you are better than this. You can achieve financial independence in ways you can be proud of and inspire others to do similarly.

Focusing on Schooling

Prioritizing academics can offer profound long-term benefits. A solid academic record can open doors to prestigious colleges and scholarships, leading to advanced career opportunities and potentially higher lifetime earnings. Furthermore, school environments provide a unique social setting for personal development and networking, where you can build lifelong relationships and gain exposure to various cultural and extracurricular activities.

If you want to go to college but you and your family cannot afford it, there is still a way for you to go. There is financial aid, scholarships, and grants. There are work study programs once you are in college. So, *don't rule college out just because you cannot afford it.* We will talk about this more in a later chapter.

However, focusing exclusively on academics means missing out on the immediate financial benefits of working and the practical skills that employment provides. It could also lead to a lack of understanding about the value of money, budgeting, and personal financial management— skills that are crucial for financial independence.

Another issue with focusing on college is that it assumes you want to attend college. Everyone should focus on having a solid high school education and a realistic action plan to achieve their goals. However, *college is not for everyone.* See the section above on "What is the big deal about going to college"?

Balancing Work and School

Many teens find themselves needing to juggle work and school. This path requires excellent time management and prioritization skills but can offer some benefits. Earning money and doing well in school can provide both immediate financial support and long-term benefits. It helps build a strong work ethic and the ability to balance multiple responsibilities. These qualities are highly valued in higher education, employment, and business.

The key to successfully managing both is setting clear priorities and boundaries. You and your employer need to agree on your school commitments. This will help you maintain a manageable schedule.

If you don't have a sense of balance between work and school, you can feel overwhelmed and want to quit. Quitting school and work would be a terrible decision. *Even if you don't want to go to college, you really need to finish high school with a solid education.*

Working Teens: Jobs, Gigs, and Side Hustles

Jobs
Finding the right part-time job can be a game-changer. Retail positions, for example, often offer flexible hours suitable for students. A job in tutoring, on the other hand, not only provides income but also helps reinforce your own knowledge. This can improve your academic performance. Food service jobs teach time management, customer interaction, and teamwork—invaluable skills in any career. When searching for these opportunities, local job boards, school career centers, and websites like Indeed.com can be great resources. Crafting a tailored resume that highlights your academic achievements, extracurricular

activities, and any volunteer experiences is crucial. Your cover letter should reflect your enthusiasm for the job and how it fits into your long-term educational goals.

Preparing for job interviews is another critical step. Dress appropriately for the role you are applying for. Neat and professional attire often makes a good first impression. Practice answering common interview questions such as "What are your strengths?" or "Why do you want to work here?" Focus your answers on how the job aligns with your school schedule and career aspirations. Demonstrating professionalism and a strong work ethic during the interview can significantly increase your chances of getting hired.

Study the following articles for more information:
- *"A Look at the Best Places to Find a Job"*[xv]
- *"Interview Tips for Teens"*[xvi]
- *"Top 10 Tips for Teens Completing Job Applications"*[xvii]
- *"How to Make a Resume for Teens with Examples"*[xviii]

Gigs
The gig economy offers another avenue for teens to earn money. Platforms like Fiverr.com and Upwork.com provide opportunities to take on freelance projects that range from graphic design to writing and editing. These gigs often offer the flexibility to work around your school schedule. For instance, you might take a food delivery gig that allows you to work evenings or weekends. Or you may freelance for a tech startup that needs simple coding done over the week. Managing these gigs requires excellent time management skills and a commitment to maintaining high-quality work, despite juggling multiple clients or projects.

Financial management also plays a huge role here. Understanding your earnings and setting aside a portion for taxes are essential practices. Apps like Quicken and Mint can help track your earnings and expenses effectively. Study the article "16 Online Jobs for Teens to Work From Home"[xix] for more information.

Side Hustles
Turning a passion into a profitable side hustle is an exciting prospect. If you are skilled at a particular game, consider coaching other players or streaming your gameplay. Artistic talents can be monetized through platforms like Etsy.com, where you can sell your artwork or handmade crafts. The key to a successful side hustle is identifying a niche that aligns with your interests and skills and where there is enough demand to make it profitable. Planning involves market research to understand potential competitors and setting realistic prices for your products or services.

Remember that people pay you for your ability to solve their problems. This is more a matter of your skills than your knowledge. Think about it. If you had to choose, do you want someone who knows about plumbing or someone who has the skills to unclog your drain? Skills can be learned. **You don't have to love your work, but you don't want to hate your work.** Try to find what makes money and what you love the most or hate the least. Study the article "The Best Skills to Learn (As a Teen) in 2024"[xx] for more information. This article discusses learnable skills you can make money with and are in demand, like content creation, video editing, social media marketing, web design and development, graphic design, and copywriting.

Once you decide on a side hustle, setting it up involves several steps. Creating a simple business plan that outlines your goals, startup costs, and pricing strategy is crucial. Understanding the legal aspects, such as obtaining the necessary permits, business licenses, or handling copyrights, if you're producing original content, is also important. Managing your taxes is important. Marketing your side hustle can take many forms, from social media campaigns to local advertising and word-of-mouth referrals. Engaging with your community or peers can provide valuable feedback and help build a customer base.

Whichever way you decide to go, the focus should always remain on balancing these opportunities with your financial independence goals. The skills, experience, and money you gain from working should enhance, not detract from, your pursuit of financial independence.

As We Close This Chapter ...

In this chapter, we have discussed the following:

- You must decide how college fits or doesn't fit into your action plan for financial independence. College is great for some and a big distraction for others.
- You must decide how working as a teenager fit or doesn't fit into your action plan. If you decide to work, you need to work on managing your time and energy so that you can at least finish high school, even if you don't want to go to college. If you want to go to college, you have extracurricular activities to consider.
- Jobs, gigs, and side hustles can be sources of income.

So, we have talked about "making money as a teenager." But what about making money after high school? The next chapter will discuss "earning high" after high school. But first, let's work through the following review and reflection questions:

Review Questions
1. A. List two of the biggest reasons to focus on going to college and two of the biggest reasons not to focus on college.

B. Can a person end up with a college degree and not be financially independent? _____ Can a person be financially independent without having a college degree? _____

C. Focusing on making money can help you earn some money, but it can come at the expense of not giving your high school education the attention that it needs. True or False   .

D. Focusing on schooling can position you for college, but it can mean not having money in your pocket and not having the skills acquired from working. True or False

E. Working while attending high school may be a good option, if you balance both.
True or False

2. Three ways for teens to make money include a j ___, g ___, and having a s ____ h ____.

Reflection Questions:
1. Consider three teenagers, each facing a decision that could influence their financial plans. Reflect on these scenarios and decide which option each teenager should choose. Explain your answer based on the principles discussed in this chapter.

A. Nia: She is 16 years old and plans to go to college. Her mother has told her that no money has been set aside for her college expenses. Nia has the opportunity to work at a local hardware store, which would involve weekend shifts that would clash with her cheerleading at school functions. The job offers her a chance to save for college, but she is also passionate about her friends and cheerleading. *What do you think Nia should do? Explain.*

B. Sophia: She is 17 years old and wants to go to college to be a professional graphic designer. She is such a talented graphic designer that she has started receiving freelance project offers through an online platform. However, her schoolwork is becoming more demanding, and she's concerned that taking on more projects might affect her grades. *What do you think Sophia should do? Explain.*

C. Brandon: He is 15 years old and wants to drive over the road trucks after high school. He then wants to own his own trucking company like his uncle. He has been offered two summer jobs: one at a café and another as a laundry attendant at his aunt's laundromat. The café job pays more immediately, but working for his aunt offers him valuable experience in how business works (but for less pay than the café job). *What do you think Brandon should do? Explain.*

2. A. If you want to attend college today, can you change your mind? If you don't want to attend college today, can you change your mind?

B. What do you want to do regarding college, as of today? Explain.

C. How does working as a teenager fit into your plans? Explain.

D. Even if working doesn't fit into your plans, which would you lean towards – a job, a gig, or a side hustle? Explain.

Chapter 3. Earning High

As a young person standing on the cusp of adulthood, the vast horizon of career opportunities can both excite and intimidate. It is like standing at the edge of a dense forest— the paths are many, the right direction unclear, and the best tools for navigation not immediately apparent.

Remember from Chapter 1 that the four pillars of financial independence are: 1. Having a "money mindset," 2 Earning high, 3. Spending low, and 4. Investing wisely. In the last chapter, we talked about making money as a teenager. In this chapter, we will discuss "earning high." *"Earning High" means making enough money to cover your expenses and invest for your financial independence.*

Success and Satisfaction

Before we move on, let me say that as important as making money is, your satisfaction with your life is also important. Think about a spectrum. On one end is "I hate my work." On the other end is "I love my work." In the middle is "I don't hate nor love my work. I'm satisfied for now." Even as a teenager, you need to work on finding harmony between success and satisfaction.

You may need to do something unsatisfying, but it pays well until you can do better for yourself. Study the topic of "delayed gratification." However, it will be difficult for you to do anything you hate for a long time, no matter how much money you are making.

There are some things that you can learn to be satisfied with when you think about how your work fits into a larger agenda. The janitor may not enjoy cleaning the floors. However, when he thinks about the importance of germ control in the hospital, his job becomes more meaningful. And when he thinks about how his income helps support his family, he finds great satisfaction in that. Study the article "The Living Experiment: Satisfaction vs. Success"[xxi] for more discussion on this topic.

Your Aptitude, the Money, and the Demand

Your Aptitude ...

When I was nearing the end of high school, my understanding of potential careers was, at best, murky. I knew of a few traditional paths—doctor, lawyer, teacher—but the details of these professions and the many other possibilities were beyond my grasp. Today, I realize the importance of early career exploration and the critical role it plays in shaping a satisfying and financially successful future.

Ideally, "earning high" begins with understanding yourself—recognizing your strengths, interests, and natural inclinations. Aptitude tests play a crucial role in this discovery process. These assessments can help you uncover skills and talents you might not have been consciously aware of and align them with potential career paths. For instance, a high aptitude for spatial reasoning and mechanical knowledge could indicate a promising career in engineering or architecture.

You should be able to access a variety of aptitude tests through your school career center, online platforms, or professional guidance counselors. It's essential to approach these tests with an open mind and use the results as a guide, not an absolute determinant of your future. They are tools designed to match your natural abilities to fields where those abilities are in demand, thereby increasing your chances of both success and satisfaction.

Study the following articles for more information:
- *"Career Exploration and Skill Development"*[xxii]
- "Helping Your Teens with Career and Self-Discovery"[xxiii]
- "Discover Your Interests and Careers to Explore"[xxiv]

But Wait, What If I do Not Have Any Aptitudes or the Wrong Aptitudes?

It is possible that you think you have no aptitudes. If this is the case, it is more likely that you need some help understanding what your aptitudes are. If, by chance, you really do not have any aptitudes, you are young enough to develop some.

"Having the wrong aptitudes" often means your aptitudes don't lead to making a lot of money, or they are not in demand. If you find yourself in this position, you are young enough to develop profitable and in-demand aptitudes.

Start with studying the articles listed above in the aptitude section. Your school's guidance counselor, a teacher, or your Pastor may be able to point you to other resources as well.

As an adult, you will not always be in a perfect situation. Sometimes you will have to make the most out of the options that you have, even though you don't love any of the options. For example, on a scale of 1 to 5, with 5 being the best, you may have to choose between a 2 or a 3 until you get to a 4 and then a 5. Think about the person who has to do the job of drawing blood (i.e., phlebotomy technician) until they can be a nurse and then be a doctor.

Ok, Show Me the Money ...
Understanding your aptitudes (i.e., what you enjoy and are good at) is one thing; knowing how to monetize them (i.e., how to make money) is another. Each skill set has its market, some more lucrative than others. Researching current and future trends in various industries can provide insights into the most valuable skills. For example, as technology continues to advance, proficiency in coding, cybersecurity, or data analysis can open doors to high-paying roles in tech companies, even without a traditional four-year degree.

The following are three ways to research how much money you can make in various fields:
- The Bureau of Labor Statistics (bls.gov) provides salary data by area, occupation, and industry.
- Job postings: Many job posting websites include a salary range field in the posting.
- Salary search websites like Salary.com, Glassdoor.com, and Salaryexpert.com can give you helpful salary range information.

What About Demand?
You don't want to be all set up to do a job that pays well, but the demand for the job is decreasing. The demand for specific jobs fluctuates based on a number of factors, including technological advancements, economic shifts, and societal needs. It is crucial that you understand not just the current demand but also the projected future demand in your chosen fields. For instance, the healthcare industry has seen consistent growth due to an aging population, making careers in medicine, nursing, and

healthcare administration secure choices for those looking for stability.

To study demand for your field of work, browse your state government's employment website (search "your state" state employment website). Many state governments list in-demand positions and industries within the given state. And the United States Bureau of Labor Statistics (BLS.gov) lists the fastest-growing occupations.

For the record, *there is a difference between a job and a career.* A job is a role or something you do for the short term, not necessarily for the long term. A career is made up of jobs, education, and all that goes into achieving your long-term goals. For example, you may have a summer job working in a restaurant, but it doesn't mean you are pursuing a career as an executive chef. You can have a summer job working at a restaurant and pursue a career in software development or being a criminal prosecutor.

Occupational Trends to Consider

Staying informed about major occupational trends is vital for making informed career choices. Here are seven significant trends that you should consider:

1. Healthcare Expansion: As mentioned, an aging population has led to increased demand in all sectors of healthcare, from direct patient care to administrative support.[xxv]

2. Green Jobs: With a global push towards sustainability, careers in environmental science, clean energy, and sustainable agriculture are becoming more prevalent and necessary.[xxvi]

3. Technology: Technology is being embedded into every aspect of life and work. Professions requiring expertise in AI, machine learning, robotics, and virtual reality are expanding.[xxvii]

4. Gig Economy: The rise of freelance work and the gig economy offers flexible career paths that didn't exist a decade ago. Skills in digital platforms, remote communication, and self-management are valuable here (see endnote xxvii).

5. Data: Data analytics and big data are revolutionizing business operations. Skills in these areas are increasingly sought after across multiple industries (see endnote xxvii).

6. Aging Population Needs: Beyond healthcare, other sectors like leisure, finance, and legal services tailored to the over 60-year-old demographic are expanding.[xxviii]

7. Educational Services: As education continues to evolve, there is a growing need for educational professionals in non-traditional settings, such as online tutors and e-learning developers (see endnote xxvi).

Confidence and Course Changes

Gaining hands-on experience through internships, shadowing professionals in fields of interest, part-time jobs, and/or apprenticeships can provide clarity and *confidence* in your career choice. It also enhances your resume and makes you a more competitive candidate in the job market or business opportunity.

The job market is continuously evolving, and staying adaptable through ongoing education and skill development is vital for your long-term career success and financial independence. What seems like such a solid decision today can be so outdated in five years. So, stay up to date with the latest developments in your field.

Let me share two things about "changing course." On one hand, if you decide on a course of action today and find a better course next year, you can *change course.* Do not be afraid to change your course from going to a good destination when you have researched and discovered a better one. Give yourself permission to change your mind, especially in light of how you are subject to learn new information as time goes along.

But on the other hand, you don't want to keep changing course without having a great reason to do so. If you are not careful, you can end up like Marvin. He started college to be an accountant. After two years, he changed course. He spent two and a half years focused on being an electrical engineer. Then, he changed course when he heard about civil engineering. He invested two and a half years focused on civil engineering, and then he concluded that engineering was not really for him. He was very frustrated and disappointed with where he was in life. He spent 7 years, accumulated over $100,000 in debt, and is still unclear about what he wants to do with his life. He may not have loved it, but at least he would be doing something that he found some satisfaction in, if he had stayed with his first or second choice.

So, if you have done your research and found something that is definitely better than what you are working on right now, sometimes pivoting from a good plan to a great plan is a wise move. But there are other times when you should simply stay the course. You can always add skills, degrees, or courses, after you have achieved some financial stability in life and are carrying out an action plan aimed at your financial independence.

7 Paths to Consider

There is no one-size-fits-all with "earning high." The following are seven of the many options you should at least look at:

1. College. Many people pursue a college degree. However, it is crucial to weigh this decision against the financial investment it requires. College costs have soared over the years, leaving many graduates burdened with substantial debt. Therefore, when considering college, compare the tuition and other associated costs against the potential income of your chosen field. For instance, careers in medicine or engineering may offer returns that justify the upfront costs of education. But the calculation might not stack up favorably in fields with lower earning potential. It is also essential to align your field of study with your passions and career aspirations to ensure long-term satisfaction and success.

2. Vocational Training. Vocational training or learning a trade can be a highly lucrative route. Trades such as electrician, plumber, or HVAC technician do not require a four-year degree and often provide on-the-job training. The benefits include entering the workforce faster and with less debt than college graduates. However, one must consider the physical demands and the potential for automation affecting some trades. To explore this path, vocational schools and community colleges offer programs where you can gain certifications and hands-on experience in various trades. These institutions often provide guidance and resources to help prospective students understand the landscape and opportunities within specific trades.

3. Truck Driving. Being a professional truck driver presents a practical option for those looking to enter the workforce quickly. With a relatively short training period, usually a few months, you can start earning a solid income, often between $50,000 and $75,000 annually. Moreover, it does not entail accumulating student debt. However, this career path can be demanding, with long hours, significant time away from home, and the physical strain of long periods of driving. Those interested can learn more through certified truck driving schools that offer courses and provide resources on licensing requirements.

4. Certificates and Two-Year Degrees. For those leaning towards a shorter educational commitment, pursuing a certificate or a two-year degree can lead to rewarding careers in various fields, including healthcare, technology, and administrative services. These programs are typically less costly than a four-year degree and require less time, allowing quicker entry into the workforce. However, the trade-off can be that the roles you get with these credentials may pay less than the roles you would get with a four-year degree. Community colleges and technical schools are excellent resources for exploring these options, offering detailed information on the scope of courses, potential career paths, and financial considerations.

You can earn a certificate or two-year degree as a milestone towards a four-year degree (or beyond) or a business opportunity. Think about how if you have a two-year degree, you at least have a degree. If you have three years of a four-year degree accomplished, you have not completed a degree.

5. The Military. Considering a career in the military is another viable path. It offers structured training, a steady income, and benefits like healthcare and tuition assistance for further education. The experience gained can be invaluable and provide a solid foundation for various roles within and outside the military. If you decide to join the military, as a United States Air Force veteran, *I urge you to try to do something in the military that you can also do when you get out.* However, this path requires significant commitment and comes with the risks associated with service. Potential recruits can gain insights from local recruitment officers who provide detailed information on the expectations and benefits of a military career.

6. Entrepreneurship. Entrepreneurship presents a dynamic avenue for those inclined towards creating and managing their own business ventures. Starting a business can be immensely rewarding, offering the potential for significant financial returns and the autonomy to make strategic decisions. However, it involves risk and requires a robust skill set including creativity, perseverance, and strategic planning. The digital landscape offers numerous opportunities for entrepreneurship, from launching an online store to providing freelance services. Aspiring entrepreneurs can leverage platforms like Amazon to publish books or Etsy to sell handmade goods. Those interested in financial markets might consider trading stocks or options, which involves understanding market dynamics and risk management.

For those exploring entrepreneurial pursuits, numerous online courses and workshops can provide the foundational knowledge and skills needed to start and grow a business. Additionally, local business incubators and online communities offer support and networking opportunities that can be crucial in the early stages of setting up a business.

7. Job. You may be in a situation where you need to make as much money as you can, right now. You don't have any time or money to invest in preparing yourself to do anything.

Let me share two things with you. On one hand, you know your situation. There is no shame in working at a fast-food restaurant for minimum wage, if that is the best you can do for now. *Sometimes, you have to do what you have to do, until you can do what you want to do.*

But on the other hand, I urge you to keep working on your "money mindset." Don't let your current situation make you think that you can only do what you are doing right now. There are thousands of stories about people who have worked their way from rags to riches, especially in America.

Career Journal

Journaling can be extremely beneficial to your carrying out your action plan. We will talk about this more in a later chapter. With your career journal, consider including the following:

- Weekly Insights: Dedicate a page a week to write down new things you learn about different careers.
- Skills Inventory: Create a section listing your skills as you discover them through aptitude tests or personal reflection.
- Industry Research: Dedicate a portion of the journal to insights from your research on different industries and how they align with your skills.
- Experience Log: Record any internships, part-time jobs, or volunteer experiences and what skills you gained or improved.

As We Close This Chapter ...

In this chapter, we have discussed the following:

- Your aptitude, the money, and the demand. Work on positioning yourself to use your aptitudes (you may have to develop new ones) in areas that pay well and are in demand.
- You should be familiar with the 7 occupational trends listed above and stay updated with changes that are sure to come.
- You should consider the 7 paths/options regarding what to do after high school and make a wise decision. Remember that sometimes you have to do what you have to do until you can do what you want to do.

So, we talked about "earning high." But what about spending money. In the next chapter, we will discuss "spending low." But first, let's work through the following review and reflection questions:

Review Questions:
1. A. In the first section of this chapter, we talked about your a _____, the m ___, and the d ____.

   B. You are given practical ways to find more information about your aptitude, the money, and the demand. True or False

   C. If you have the wrong aptitude or no aptitude, you are doomed. True or False

2. A. How many occupational trends are listed above?

   B. Is being a YouTuber listed as one of the occupational trends?

C. After the practical discussion of how to gain confidence about your decision, I tell you to stay with your decision, no matter what. True or False.

3. A. How many paths are you asked to consider?

B. If you don't choose college, does that mean you are not smart enough to go to college?

C. Is it possible to make good money without having a college degree?

Reflection Questions:
1. As you reflect on the following scenarios, discuss which paths might suit each individual best based on their interests, skills, and financial situations. What are the potential risks and rewards associated with each option?

- Maria has always excelled in science and math. She's considering taking on student loans to attend a prestigious university and study biomedical engineering—a field that promises high future earnings but requires significant upfront investment in education.

- Jake enjoys working with his hands and fixing things. He's torn between attending a four-year college as his parents wish or pursuing a certification in HVAC systems, which could lead to immediate employment and income without substantial debt.

- Lily has a flair for digital design and social media. She's debating whether to go to college for graphic design or start her own online business creating digital content for companies.

2. A. Given what you know today, what are you leaning towards doing after high school to "earn high"?

B. What are 3-5 steps you need to take to get to where you want to go?

C. What are some resources that you need to study and people you need to talk to about what you are trying to do?

D. When will you study the first resource and talk to the first person?

E. How are you doing with your "money mindset" work (knowledge, plan, and grit)?

Chapter 4. Spending Low

Imagine Sarah, a bright and ambitious teenager with a part-time job, staring at her bank statement in frustration. Despite her earnings, her account balance is alarmingly low. She has been overspending on clothes and outings with friends, and now the reality of her dwindling savings is setting in. This scenario is common and highlights the critical role of budgeting in your quest for financial independence.

Financial independence is not just about how much you earn. More importantly, it is about how you manage what you earn. Earning $100,000 annually means little if you also spend $100,000. You may be more comfortable, but you are as broke as someone who makes $50,000 a year and spends it all.

Remember from Chapter 1 that the four pillars of financial independence are: 1. Having a "money mindset," 2. Earning high, 3. Spending low, and 4. Investing wisely. In the last chapter, we discussed "earning high." In this chapter, we will discuss "spending low." *"Spending Low" means controlling your spending so that you have enough income to invest for your financial independence.*

Your Money Personality

Understanding your financial behaviors starts with identifying your "money personality." Think of the following four money personalities: spenders, savers, investors, and givers. Each type influences your financial decisions, from daily spending to long-term investing.

Spenders often enjoy the immediate gratification of purchasing and prioritize current desires over saving for the future. While this can make them feel momentarily happy, it might lead to financial strain, if not balanced with a budget. Budgeting is essential for spenders to have enough money to save and invest for financial independence. They may also need to be encouraged to give to help others.

Savers take comfort in the security that comes from having money set aside. They are less likely to spend impulsively and often have funds ready for emergencies. Savers may need encouragement to spend some of their money and to give to help others. They may also need to be pushed to understand the difference between saving and investing.

Investors continuously seek ways to use their money to generate more income. They are usually willing to take calculated risks for potential returns. Investors may need encouragement to spend some of their money and to give to help others. They may also need to be reminded to save some money in an emergency fund, instead of having all their money invested.

Givers prioritize using their finances to help others. They may donate to churches, charities, support family members, or invest in community projects. Givers may need some encouragement to spend some of their money on themselves. Budgeting is crucial for givers to have enough money to save and invest for financial independence.

How do you see yourself? Are you more of a spender, saver, investor, or giver? Understanding your money personality is a huge step in the right direction. Next, you need to make the necessary adjustments.

It is alright to be a spender, if you spend within your budget. Your budget should include allocations for savings, investing, and helping others. It is okay to be a saver, if your budget includes allocations for investing, enjoying some of your money, and helping others. It is alright to be an investor, if your budget includes allocations for savings (e.g., emergency fund and big purchases), enjoying some of your money, and helping others. And it is great to be a giver, if your budget includes allocations for saving, investing, and enjoying some of your money.

7 Things to Keep in Mind

As a teenager, there are some things that you need to have some familiarity with, but you don't need to be an expert on the topics. Here are seven things that fit into that category:

1. Emotional Spending. Emotions play a significant role in financial decisions, often driving spending habits more than we might realize. The excitement of a new purchase or the status boost from owning popular brands can overshadow practical considerations like affordability or necessity. This emotional spending is further amplified by the 'fear of missing out,' or FOMO, a prevalent feeling among teens influenced by social media and peer activities. Managing these emotions requires mindfulness and strategies to pause and reflect before making financial commitments. Asking yourself whether a purchase is driven by need or a temporary desire can help you make more reasoned financial choices.

2. Needs vs. Wants. Distinguishing between needs and wants is a fundamental skill in effective money management. Needs are essentials, such as food, housing, and basic transportation, that you must budget for. Wants are items or services that enhance your life but are not essential for your immediate survival. Examples of wants may be daily special coffee drinks from the coffee shop, additional shoes, and additional video games. Covering your needs first and then your most important wants as your budget allows is especially crucial when funds are limited.

3. Research. Making informed purchasing decisions goes beyond simply choosing between different brands or products. It involves researching, comparing prices, checking reviews, and considering the long-term value of a purchase. This deliberate approach helps avoid impulsive buys based on emotional impulses or peer influence. For example, suppose you want to buy a new laptop. In that case, you should compare models, check user reviews, look for discounts, and consider how long you plan to use it to determine which option offers the best value for your needs.

4. Online Banking. If you don't have a checking account yet, you should probably be working on getting one. The checking account is usually used to deposit your paychecks and write checks to pay your expenses. A savings account is often where you hold your emergency fund and money you save for large purchases. Make sure you understand the terms of the accounts, so you are not charged service fees for things like not having a large enough balance in your savings account.

Online banking is common today. You can take pictures of checks to deposit into your account, transfer money from your checking to your savings account, check balances from your phone, receive direct deposits, and so much more. Online banking can be very convenient. However, you should put some security measures in place like strong, unique passwords, two-factor authentication, and ensuring that the website or app is secure (indicated by 'https' in the web address). Unfortunately, there are many bad actors trying to steal your money from your online banking activities.

5. Taxes. No one really enjoys paying taxes. However, taxes are the way the government (i.e., federal, state, and local) pays for the services they provide to their citizens. For example, taxes are used to pay for the roads we travel on, the public schools that young people attend, libraries, police, firefighters, sheriffs, state troopers, military, Social Security, Medicare, and so much more. As a teenager, you should know that taxes are taken from your paycheck (i.e., income taxes). When you buy certain items, you pay sales tax. If you owned real estate, you would probably have to pay real estate taxes. All these taxes help fund various levels of government activities. At some point, you need to learn about strategies to lower your income taxes without being guilty of tax evasion.

6. Credit, Credit Cards, and Debt. Good *credit* can open doors to significant opportunities, such as qualifying for lower interest rates on loans, securing housing, and even influencing job prospects. Poor credit can close these doors, making it challenging to achieve financial stability. Credit scores range from 300 to 850 and are based on several factors, including payment history, amounts owed, length of credit history, new credit, and types of credit used.

As a teenager, you should work on paying any debt you owe on time. If you get a *credit card,* aim to pay it off monthly or pay as much as you can each month. This will help you with your credit score and help you not have to pay so much in credit card interest.

If you end up having *debt* (i.e., you owe more than you will pay off in one or two months), you should be familiar with *the "snowball" approach.* The following are the big ideas behind the snowball approach to paying off debt:

- List all your debts and the minimum monthly payment for each.
- Pay all the minimum monthly payments.
- Take any extra money and pay off the smallest debt.
- Take the money you used to spend on the smallest debt and any extra money and pay off the next smallest debt.
- Do this until all the debts are paid off.

Study the article "How the Debt Snowball Method Works"[xxix] for more information.

7. Insurances. Not only do people not like paying taxes, but people also don't like paying for insurance. However, when you need insurance, you will be glad you have it. In broad strokes, you pay premiums to get protection. There is *health insurance,* which will become more and more important to you as you get older. There is *car insurance.* This includes learning about liability coverage (i.e., costs associated with injury and damage to others), collision coverage (i.e., cost for damage to your vehicle), and more. With *homeowners' insurance,* the policy covers the house and possessions in the house, if something terrible happens like a fire, burglary, someone is injured on the property, etc. *Renter's insurance* covers your personal property and liability. The owner has insurance on the building. *Life insurance* may seem like it is not necessary for you. But be mindful that life insurance for someone in their teens or twenties is normally much cheaper than for someone in their 40s or 50s.

Basic Budgeting

Basic budgeting relates to your month-to-month normal income and expenses. The following are four ideas to consider in building your basic budget:

1. Income. Understand and make note of where your income is coming from and make note of how much income you expect from the various sources. For example, you may have $100/month from allowance, $450/month from your part-time job, and $100/month from your side hustle for a total income of $750/month.

2. Expenses. Understand and make note of what you *need* to spend money on (i.e., necessities) and what you want to spend money on (i.e., discretionary spending). Prioritize allocating money for your long-term goals (e.g., a car, college or training expenses, apartment, etc.) a higher priority than excessive short-term pleasure like eating out four and five times a week, three and four streaming subscriptions, and buying the newest sneakers to add to your collection.

3. The 70/30 budget. The following are the big ideas behind this budgeting concept:
- Live on 70% of your take-home income
- Use 20% of your take-home income to pay off high-interest debt, build your emergency fund, and then invest
- Use 10% of your take-home income to give to your church, charity, or something of this nature.

Study the article, "The 70/30 Rule"[xxx] for more information.

4. Envelopes, Accounts, and Websites/Apps. The *envelope* system is old-fashioned, but it works. You allocate a set amount of cash to different spending categories each month by putting the cash in an envelope. Once the money in an envelope is gone, no more spending is allowed in that category until the next month. This can be particularly effective when saving for a big purchase. It physically restricts how much you can spend, making it easier to stick to your savings plan.

Setting up a savings *account* for big purchases can be great. This psychologically separates this money from your regular spending funds, making you less likely to dip into it for other expenses. It also allows you to earn a little interest on your savings.

Websites/apps like Quicken (quicken.com), Mint (mint.intuit.com), or You Need A Budget (ynab.com) offer robust platforms that allow you to track your income and expenses, set up savings goals, and monitor your progress. These tools often sync with your bank accounts and credit cards, providing real-time insights into your spending and saving habits. They can also help you identify areas where you can cut back or optimize your spending to meet your savings targets faster. Search for "free budgeting apps for young adults."

What if My Expenses are Higher Than My Income?

Sometimes things don't work out as planned. When your expenses exceed your income, you will have to choose from the following options:

1. Cut Your Expenses. If cutting your discretionary spending will help your expenses be equal to or less than your income, that is a good place to start. With your money mindset, you must decide which is more important, spending money for non-essentials today or saving and investing for tomorrow. Even with your necessities, you should see if there are ways to pay less for them.

However, having no discretionary spending for an extended period is not sustainable. You are subject to losing your motivation to stay so disciplined. Everyone needs to have a little fun sometimes.

2. Earn More Income. This may involve working more hours, getting a better job, adding a side hustle, or other similar measures.

3. Do both. This is a combination of numbers 1 and 2 above. *Many teens and young adults will choose this option.*

4. Accumulate Debt. This is far from ideal and often a wrong choice. Accumulating debt can make you feel bad (i.e., you owe someone some money). And if interest is being applied to the debt, you can find yourself in a situation that keeps getting worse. It is bad to owe $1,000 but owing an extra $15/month is even worse (i.e., 18% annual interest).

How to Get More for Less

The following are some ideas for teenagers and young adults to consider as ways to get more out of the money that they have:

1. Clothing and Accessories. Look for sales, clearance racks, and discounts to get the most out of your budget. Invest in versatile pieces that can be mixed and matched to create multiple outfits, reducing the need for new clothes. Learn basic sewing to repair clothes. Purchase gently used clothing and accessories from thrift and consignment stores.

2. Food and Snacks. Bring homemade lunches and snacks to school, instead of buying them. Look for coupons, student discounts, and loyalty programs to save on food purchases. Learn to cook at home when possible. Crockpot meals can be tasty and cheap. Plan your meals for the week to avoid impulse buys. Limit your coffee shop visits. Brew your own coffee at home. Use a water bottle instead of buying bottled water. Reserve dining out for special occasions. Just have water when you eat out and save the money you would have otherwise spent on a beverage.

3. Entertainment. Share streaming service subscriptions with family and friends to split the cost. Look for free community events, movie nights, and other low-cost entertainment options. Borrow books, movies, and games from friends or the library, instead of buying new ones. Cancel unnecessary subscriptions or memberships.

4. Technology and Gadgets. Purchase gently used or refurbished electronics to save money. Buy gadgets during major sales events like Black Friday or back-to-school sales. Use free versions of apps and software whenever possible to avoid unnecessary spending.

5. Transportation. Take advantage of public transportation options, which are often cheaper than driving. Walk or bike for short trips. Share rides with friends to save on gas and reduce wear and tear on your vehicle. Regularly maintain your car to prevent costly repairs and improve fuel efficiency.

6. Beauty and Personal Care. Try homemade beauty treatments and skincare products, instead of expensive store-bought ones. Purchase personal care items in bulk to save money in the long run. Use the recommended amount of beauty products to make them last longer.

7. Social Activities. Organize low-cost activities like cookouts, movie nights at home, or hiking trips. Take advantage of student discounts for events and activities. Instead of going out, host potluck dinners where everyone brings a dish, reducing the overall cost. Plan no-spend weekends.

8. School Supplies and Books. Purchase used textbooks or rent them, instead of buying new ones. Use the school's library and online resources to save on book and supply costs. Buy school supplies during back-to-school sales and stock up for the year.

9. Hobbies and Interests. Borrow equipment from friends or trade items to avoid buying new ones. Take advantage of free or low-cost classes and workshops in your community. Create your own supplies or equipment for hobbies, instead of purchasing them.

10. Gifts and Charitable Donations. Create personal-ized, homemade gifts, which are often more meaningful and cost-effective. Establish a spending limit for gifts and stick to it. Pool resources with friends or family to buy one nice gift, instead of multiple smaller ones.

11. Apartment. Use energy-efficient appliances to reduce utility bills. Try to repair and repurpose rather than replace items. Avoid late fees by paying bills on time. Take shorter showers to save on water and heating. Do price comparisons before making significant purchases. Sell items you no longer need on "online marketplaces."

12. General Money Management. Track all your expenses for a month to identify where you can cut back. Use an app like Acord (acorns.com/invest) to round up your purchases and save the spare change. Take advantage of sales and clearance items. Shop with a list to avoid impulse purchases. Save bonuses or tax refunds instead of spending them.

Budgeting for Big Purchases

When considering big or significant purchases like a car, a nice trip, the latest tech gadget, or saving for your first apartment, it's wise to plan for it. The following are five things to consider:

1. Research. If you need or really want the item, research it to ensure that you get a good product or service at a reasonable price. Study your options to find quality that you can afford. Understand what a reasonable price is. Negotiate for a lower price, if you can.

2. Set Monthly Allocations. Assuming you have done your research, divide the total cost by the number of months that work for you. For example, if you need $1,500 for a new laptop and accessories, and you can afford $100/month, it will take you 15 months to save up the $1,500. If you want the computer in 6 months, you need to save $250/month. Remember the previous section about what to do when your expenses exceed your income.

3. Your First Car. Assuming you *need* a car, instead of simply wanting one, the following are some things to keep in mind:

- *Budget and Total Cost of Ownership.* Before purchasing a used car, it's crucial to establish a budget that includes the purchase price and additional costs such as *insurance, registration, maintenance, and potential repairs.* Study the articles "What Is the Total Cost of Owning a Car?" and "How Much Does It Cost to Own a Car?" for more information.[xxxi]

- *Vehicle History Report.* Obtain a vehicle history report using services like CARFAX or AutoCheck to check for any past accidents, title issues, or previous ownership details. This report can reveal red flags like flood damage, odometer rollbacks, or if the car was ever classified as salvage, which could impact its safety and reliability. Study the articles "What is a Vehicle History Report?" and "Why Run an AutoCheck Vehicle History Report?" for more information."[xxxii]

- *Pre-Purchase Inspection.* Have a trusted mechanic inspect the car before making a purchase. Even if the vehicle appears to be in good condition, there could be hidden issues that only a professional can identify. This inspection can save you from unexpected repairs and give you leverage in price negotiations. Study the articles "Why a Pre-Purchase Car Inspection Is Important" and "How to Inspect a Used Car Before Buying" for more information.[xxxiii]

- *Test Drive and Comfort.* Always take the car for a test drive to assess its performance, comfort, and handling. Pay attention to how the car feels when driving, any unusual noises, the responsiveness of the brakes, and how comfortable it is for your driving style. This hands-on experience can reveal issues that aren't apparent from just looking at the car. Study the articles "What to Look for on a Test Drive" and "The Best Way to Test Drive a Car" for more information.[xxxiv]

4. Your First Apartment. Assuming you *need* an apartment, instead of simply wanting one, the following are some things to keep in mind:

- *Budget and Affordability.* Determining how much you can realistically afford to spend on rent each month is essential. This includes considering not just the rent itself but also utilities, groceries, and other living expenses. Many landlords require that your monthly income be three times the rent, so having a clear budget is crucial to avoid financial strain. Study articles "12 Steps to Take Before Renting Your First Apartment" and "Step-by-Step Guide to Getting Your First Apartment" for more information.[xxxv]

- *Location and Amenities.* The location of your apartment will impact your daily life, including commute times, access to public transportation, and proximity to work or school. Additionally, consider what amenities are important to you, such as on-site laundry, parking, or a gym, as these can affect your comfort and convenience. Study articles "Renting an Apartment for the First Time: A Guide for New Renters" and "8 Key Tips for a First-Time Apartment Renter" for more information.[xxxvi]

- *Understand the Lease Agreement.* The lease is a legally binding document outlining your tenant rights and responsibilities. Before signing, ensure you understand the terms related to rent payments, lease length, maintenance responsibilities, and rules like subletting or having pets. Failing to fully understand your lease can lead to unexpected issues later. See end notes xxxv and xxxvi.

- *Safety and Security.* Your safety should be a top priority. When visiting potential apartments, assess the security features such as locks, lighting, and neighborhood safety. Additionally, consider renters insurance, which can protect you in case of apartment theft, damage, or accidents. See end notes xxxvi.

5. Adjusting to the Unexpected. When doing basic month-to-month budgeting and planning for big purchases, it is essential to be realistic and brace for the unexpected. Don't frustrate yourself by projecting income you cannot count on.

And then life can be unpredictable. Income that you thought you would have may not happen. Your job can let you go. Your side hustle doesn't pay off as expected. And expenses that you did not anticipate can pop up. There can be an emergency around the house, your clothes can be destroyed by someone spilling paint on them, or any number of things.

The best you can do is the best you can do. Don't stress over things beyond your control. If you must stop saving for a while, do what you have to do. And get back to your plan as soon as you can.

Financial Planning for College

Even though tuition can be rather expensive, unfortunately, it is not the only expense related to college. There can be room and board (i.e., housing and meals), books and supplies, codes to platforms, lab fees, transportation, personal care items, leisure activities, etc. If you are focusing on college, research and learn about all the expenses you will need to cover. You can study the college website, attend college fairs, talk to college advisors, and visit campuses to help with your research.

71

While you are researching, you should consider the following three ideas:

1. Online Schools. They can offer significant savings on room and board and commuting costs. They provide flexible learning environments, often ideal for students needing to work while studying or who prefer a non-traditional learning environment. However, it's crucial to ensure that the online school has proper accreditation and that its courses are recognized by employers or other educational institutions, if further education is anticipated.

2. Historically Black Colleges and Universities (HBCUs). They offer culturally enriched environments and are often praised for their supportive communities. They tend to be smaller, which can translate to more personalized attention and support from faculty and staff. Prospective students should consider the school's academic offerings to ensure they align with their career goals.

3. Community Colleges. They present another viable option, especially for students looking to ease the financial burden of a four-year degree. They offer lower tuition rates and the opportunity to transfer credits to a four-year university later, which can significantly reduce the total cost of education. Students must carefully research transfer agreements to ensure their credits will be accepted by the four-year institution they plan to attend.

Ways to Pay for College

If you don't have any money for school, don't despair. The following are three ways to pay for college:

1. Savings. Traditional savings accounts offer a safe place to accumulate funds over time, but the interest earned is often minimal. More strategic options include 529 plans and Education Savings Accounts (ESAs), both of which offer tax advantages to encourage saving for education. While 529 plans are operated by states and come with high contribution limits, ESAs provide the flexibility to be used for primary and secondary education expenses as well as college costs. Each has its benefits and limitations, and choosing the right one depends on individual financial situations and educational goals.

2. Scholarships and Grants. These provide an opportunity to fund education without the burden of repayment, making them highly attractive options. They can be based on various criteria including academic merit, athletic talent, cultural heritage, or field of study. High school counselors can be invaluable resources in identifying scholarship opportunities, as can websites like Fastweb.com and Scholarships.com, which allow students to search for scholarships based on their qualifications and interests.

3. Financial Aid. Applying for financial aid through the Free Application for Federal Student Aid (FAFSA) is essential for any student needing financial assistance. The FAFSA determines eligibility for federal grants, loans, and work-study funds. It is used by many states and schools for their own financial aid programs. Submitting the FAFSA as early as possible is crucial as many awards are given on a first-come, first-served basis.

Crafting robust applications for scholarships and grants involves more than just meeting eligibility criteria. It requires thoughtful preparation and attention to detail. Start by thoroughly reading application instructions and gathering all necessary documents. Essays are a common requirement and should be crafted to meet and exceed the selection criteria. They should tell a compelling story, be meticulously proofread, and be tailored to each application. Letters of recommendation also play a critical role. They should be sought from individuals who can provide meaningful insights into your abilities and character.

As We Close This Chapter ...

In this chapter, we have discussed the following:
- You should understand your money personality. If you are more like a spender, saver, investor, or giver simply make the necessary adjustments.
- Under the 7 things to keep in mind, we discussed emotional spending, needs vs. wants, researching before purchasing, online banking, taxes; credit, credit cards, and debt; and insurances.
- Under basic budgeting, we discussed income, expenses, the 30/70 budget, and envelopes, accounts, and websites/apps.
- What if my expenses are higher than my income? We discussed the four options.
- Under how to get more for less, I shared tips on 12 common areas where teenagers and young adults spend their money.
- Under budgeting for big purchases, we discussed researching, setting monthly allocations, your first car, and your first apartment. We talked about adjusting to the unexpected.
- Under financial planning for college, we discussed online schools, historically Black colleges and universities, and community colleges.
- Under ways to pay for college, we talked about savings, scholarships and grants, and financial aid.

So, we have discussed "spending low." But when are we going to talk about financial independence? In the next chapter, we will discuss "investing wisely." But before we do so, let's work through the following review and reflection questions:

Review Questions:
1. A. What are the four pillars of financial independence?

B. What are the four money personalities? If you are a spender or giver, does that mean you are wrong and cannot reach financial independence?

2. A. How many things to keep in mind were discussed?

B. What does FOMO stand for?

C. What are taxes used for?

D. What approach is discussed to pay off debt?

3. A. With budgeting, you need to understand and make note of both your i _____ sources and e _____.

B. What is the 70/30 Budget?

C. Sometimes you may have to cut some e _____ and boost your i _____ to make your budget work.

4. A. You were given some tips on how many different areas of spending?

B. Does every teenager *need* a car and apartment?

C. When you make a budget for your regular month-to-month or big purchases, things will always work out as planned. True or False

5. With financial planning for college, there are no other ways to pay for college, except you saving enough money to pay for it. True or False

Reflection Questions:
1. Which money personality do you see yourself as? Explain. What adjustments do you need to make?

2. If you receive a monthly allowance of $100, earn $300/m from your part-time job, and make $100/m from your social media management side hustle, what is your total monthly income? If you usually spend $300/m on things like clothes, food, entertainment, etc., how much do you have left over? How much can you budget for big purchases, savings, and investing altogether? If you want to save and invest $300/m, what are your options?

3. If you are focused on going to college, which way of paying for it are you leaning towards? Explain.

4. How are you doing with your "money mindset" work (knowledge, plan, and grit)?

A Quick Question ...

.... If you could help a teenager, in 60 seconds and at no cost to you, would you?

If I can get this book, **Money Management for Teens**, into the hands of teenagers, it will help them greatly.

Research shows that before a person looks inside the book, they look at the cover and number of reviews. I need you to leave a review so that when others consider this book, they will see many reviews. You can leave a review in 60 seconds and at no cost to you.

Your review can help teenagers see that no matter where they are now, they can take control of their lives and be the first (or next) financially independent person in their family.

Your review can help teenagers see that even though college may not be for them, financial independence is still possible.

Your review can help a parent or caregiver purchase this book for teenagers in their lives.

All you have to do is scan the QR code below to leave your review:

Thank YOU so much.

Fun fact: If you provide something of value to another person, it makes you more valuable to them. If you believe this book will help a teenager, send them a copy.

Chapter 5. Investing Wisely

Imagine a teenager, let's call him Jordan, who has just received his first paycheck from a summer job. He was thrilled to see his own money in his bank account. Yet, as he thinks about his newfound finances, he faces a crucial decision: should he spend his earnings on a new gaming console that he has been eyeing, or should he save and invest his money for future gains? This is a pivotal moment for Jordan. The habits he forms now could set the foundation for his financial future.

Remember from Chapter 1 that the four pillars of financial independence are: 1. Having a "money mindset," 2. Earning high, 3. Spending low, and 4. Investing wisely. In the last chapter, we discussed "spending low." In this chapter, we will discuss "investing wisely." ***"Investing wisely" means allocating resources towards assets that help you reach financial independence.***

Saving

Saving money means putting money into something like a savings account. The goal is *not* to make a lot of money from what you put into savings. *The goal is to have a sum of money at some point in the future.* Two major reasons to save money are to have an emergency fund and to have make a big purchase.

An *emergency fund* is having at least 3-6 months of your living expenses in something like a savings account. For example, if your living expenses are $3,000/month, you should have an emergency fund of $9,000 to $18,000.

This means that if you lose your job, the money from your side hustle drops, or you run into an unexpected expense (e.g., car repair, increase in rent, family emergency, etc.), you can respond without having to buy stuff on a high-interest credit card or taking out a loan.

As for *big purchases* like a car, paying for a training program, college expenses, or a computer, having money in a savings account can help you make the purchase without paying the interest associated with a credit card or a loan. However, you must exercise the discipline and patience needed to save the money to make the purchase.

Investing

Investing means buying **something at a low price that you plan to sell at a higher price** (i.e., appreciation) like a stock or a business. Or you may be **buying something that you expect to give you money regularly in the future** (i.e., cash flow) like dividends from a stock, royalties from a digital product, or rent from real estate.

The goal of investing is to one day have enough money coming in from your investments to cover your living expenses. Instead of working for money and paying your bills, you receive money from your investments to pay your bills. This is financial independence and the goal of being a wise investor.

Four Key Concepts

You need to be familiar with the following four key concepts, as you think about and take action in the areas of saving and investing:

1. Inflation. The rate of inflation is essentially the rate of your dollar losing its purchasing power. An inflation rate of 3% means that on the last day of the year, your dollar is worth 3% less than it was on the first day of the year. For example, in January you may be able to buy a pair of AirForce Ones for $120. But at a 3% inflation rate, in December, the same sneakers may cost about $124.

You need to keep inflation in mind, because it works against your goal of financial independence. If you make a 10% return on your investment, but the inflation rate is 3%, your net return is only 7%. If you make a 3% return on your savings account and inflation is 3%, your net is 0%. If you keep your money in your dresser drawer and inflation is at 3%, your net is -3%. Remember that you need your money to grow because inflation is working against you.

2. Risk vs. Reward. Essentially, the more reward you receive from an investment, the more risk you will typically have to take. And the safer an investment is, the less reward you will normally receive. For example, putting your money into a savings account is pretty safe (very low risk), and the reward is very low (i.e., at the time of this writing, some banks were only paying about .5% with an inflation rate of 3%). On the other hand, investing in a stock can produce a 20% return on your investment (i.e., you put in $100 in January, and it is worth $120 in December) – high reward. But there is a high risk. Not only can the rate of return be lower than 20%, but you can also lose some or all the money you put into the investment.

So, you need to think about your "risk tolerance." If you have a low-risk tolerance, you may have a safe set of investments (i.e., portfolio) but a low return on investment. If you have a high-risk tolerance, you *may* have a high return on investment or a lower return. You may even lose some or all the money that you invested in the first place.

If you have a moderate risk tolerance, you are trying to take the best of both extremes and avoid the worst of both extremes. You are aiming for a decent return on your investments without losing the money that you put into the investment. To be a bit clearer, if a 3% return on investment is what low-risk tolerance investors seek and 20% is what high-risk tolerance investors seek, a moderate-risk investor may seek something around 10%.

3. Diversification. This concept is about putting your money into more than one investment. If you put all your money into one investment and it fails then your entire portfolio has failed. But if you put your money in several investments, even if one investment fails, the other investments may be doing well enough to keep you moving towards your goals.

4. Compounding Interest. Often this is referred to as the "eighth wonder of the world" by financial enthusiasts. Compound interest is when interest is added to the initial principal, and then additional interest is earned on the accumulated interest. This snowball effect can turn even modest savings into substantial sums over an extended period.

Imagine you invest $1,000 at an interest rate of 12% annually. At the end of the first year, you don't just have your initial $1,000 but an additional $120 in interest, totaling $1,120. In the second year, interest is calculated on the new total of $1,120, resulting in another $134.40 in interest, and so on. Over 20 years, this initial sum can grow to $9,646 without any additional deposits.

In your continued studies, you may run across the "Rule of 72." Essentially, the concept is that if you divide 72 by the rate of return you are considering, the result is how many years it will take for your money to double. For example, at a rate of 8%/year, your money would double in 9 years (72/8). At a rate of 10%/year, your money would double in 7.1 years (72/10).

Compounding interest is your friend when you are looking at your investments. When you are investing, you want a high interest rate. However, it is your enemy when you are paying interest on a loan like a credit card. When paying interest, you want the interest rate to be as low as possible.

5 Rather Traditional Investment Strategies

There are many investment strategies. The following are five rather traditional investment strategies that you should be familiar with:

1. Bonds. Bonds are loans you, as the investor, give to an entity like the government or a corporation. In return for your loan, the issuing entity promises to pay back the principal amount on a specified maturity date and make regular interest payments during the life of the bond. Bonds would be an example of low risk and low return. Study the article "How to Invest in Bonds,"[xxxvii] for more information.

2. Stocks. Stocks are essentially you owning a piece of a corporation like Amazon, Microsoft, Tesla, etc. When the value of the stock goes up, you make money on your investment. When the value of the stock goes down, you lose money. Some stocks have dividends, where you keep your stock, but you get paid to hold the stock.

Let's say you purchase a stock for $100 and the value rises to $110. You just made $10, if you sell at $110 (i.e., appreciation). Let's say you purchased it for $100, and the value dropped to $90. You lose $10, if you sell at $90 (i.e., deprecation). Notice that you must buy and sell to experience a net gain or loss.

With dividends, if you purchase a stock for $100 and it pays a dividend each year of $5 (i.e., cash flow), the $5 is yours if the value of the stock goes up to $110 or drops to $90. With cash flow, you keep the stock.

Even though you can make great money with stocks and even with dividends. You need to develop the appropriate knowledge about stock selection, decide which platform to purchase the stocks from, and then exercise the discipline and patience to carry out your plan, despite the values going up and down (i.e., volatility). Furthermore, you can lose some or all your initial investment in the stock. This is often a high-reward and high-risk situation. Study the article "Stock Market Basics: 9 Tips for Beginners"[xxxviii] for more information.

3. Cryptocurrency. This is a digital or virtual currency that uses cryptography for security. Unlike traditional currencies issued by governments (like the US dollar or euro), cryptocurrencies operate on technology called blockchain. This decentralized technology allows cryptocurrencies to work without a central authority like a bank or government. Two of the biggest positives of cryptocurrency investing are that it can offer high returns and that anyone with an internet connection can invest (i.e., accessibility). Some negatives are that prices can fluctuate wildly (i.e., high-risk), a lack of regulations (which means fraud and scams can happen), and understanding how cryptocurrencies and blockchain technology work can be complicated for beginners. Study the article "Start Investing in Cryptocurrency: A Guide for Newcomers & Beginners"[xxxix] for more information.

4. Mutual Funds. Think of mutual funds as a group of stocks and/or bonds that are managed by a fund manager (i.e., an expert in stocks and bonds). On one hand, you can make money by using the fund manager's expertise. But on the other hand, the fund manager may not do well. In fact, the fund manager can do a bad job, and you still pay them. This is less risk and less reward than you trying to pick and manage your own stocks. Study the article "How To Invest in Mutual Funds"[xl] for more information.

5. Exchange Traded Funds (i.e., ETFs). Think of the 500 largest stocks in America. Instead of picking one or two, you can own all of them by owning a share of the exchange traded fund. ETFs tend to cost less than mutual funds and often perform better than mutual funds. This strategy can be less risky than a mutual fund and a little more rewarding.

I personally invest in ETFs. They allow the average person to invest in stocks without being an expert or paying for one. For my grandchildren, I invest one-third of their money in the S&P 500 (i.e., the 500 largest stocks in the United States, VOO), one-third in dividend corporations (i.e., SCHD), and one-third in large growth stocks (i.e., SCHG).

In your studies, you will come across the term "asset allocation." It is very similar to the idea of diversification. When you are younger, you can invest in more growth and risk. When you are closer to living on the income from your investments, you may want to focus more on dividends and fundamental stocks. Study the article "How to Invest in ETFs"[xli] for more information.

Investment Simulators and Financial Advisors

Investment simulators are tools or platforms that allow individuals to practice investing in bonds, stocks, cryptocurrency, mutual funds, and exchange traded funds without using real money. These simulators mimic real-world financial markets and investment scenarios, helping users learn about investing in a risk-free environment. They can help you develop your confidence and evaluate your investment strategies. Search "Investopedia Simulator" and "MarketWatch Virtual Stock Exchange" for more information about investment simulators.

Financial advisors are professionals who provide advice and guidance on managing finances, including investments, savings, retirement planning, and more. When you are ready to put $50,000 or more into the market, you may want to contact a financial advisor. They help individuals create and implement financial plans to achieve their goals. When choosing a financial advisor, you want to see credentials like Certified Financial Planner (CFP) or Chartered Financial Analyst (CFA). Understand how the advisor charges for their services. Some charge a flat fee, others a percentage of assets managed, or commissions. Research the advisor's experience and reputation. Reading reviews and asking for referrals can provide insights into their reliability, expertise, and compatibility with your goals. Studying a book like this one will help you have an informed conversation with a financial advisor.

What If You Only Have $5 and Spare Change?

Micro-investing apps allow you to buy pieces (i.e., fractions) of a share of stock or ETF. Research platforms like Acorns (i.e., round up everyday purchases to the nearest dollar, invest your spare change, and educational resources), Stash (i.e., start with as little as $5 and educational resources), and Robinhood (i.e. start investing with as little as $1 and educational resources). If you were my grandchild, I would tell you to look at getting started with one of these and do better when you learn better.

Non-Traditional Investment Strategies

The above were rather traditional strategies. The following are two non-traditional strategies for investing:

1. Real Estate. There are many ways to make money with real estate. You can buy real estate (e.g., land, houses, apartments, buildings, etc.) at a low price and sell for a high price (i.e., appreciation). You can buy real estate and rent or lease it to others (i.e., producing cash flow). You can purchase shares of a real estate investment trust (i.e., REIT). With a REIT, you can invest in significant real estate deals one share at a time, similar to buying a share of an ETF and owning a portion of thousands of properties. Study the article "Investing in REITs for Beginners"[xlii] for more information.

There is also the idea of *house hacking*. House hacking is a strategy where an investor purchases a property and lives in part of it, while renting out other parts to generate income. This income can help cover the mortgage and other property-related expenses. It is a popular method for young investors, including teenagers, to get started in real estate with limited funds. Study the article "A Guide to House Hacking with a Fourplex"[xliii] for more information.

2. Business Ownership. Investing in business ownership can mean you start, buy, or invest in a business to generate income and/or potentially sell the business for a profit in the future. You may want to consider turning your side hustle into a business that you grow and then sell. You can grow the business and hire people to do the work while you enjoy the cash flow. With the internet and modern advances, you can start an online business that grows into a significant part of your action plan for financial independence. Research topics like earning royalties from digital products (e.g., ebooks, online courses, etc.), affiliate marketing, peer-to-peer lending, and investing in dividend-yielding stocks.

As We Close This Chapter ...

In this chapter, we have discussed the following:
- With savings, we talked about having an emergency fund and saving money for big purchases.
- With investing, we talked about inflation, risk vs. reward, diversification, and compounding interest.
- With the five traditional investment strategies, we looked at bonds, stocks, cryptocurrency, mutual funds, exchange traded funds, ETFs, and how to start with only $5 and spare change. We also mentioned investment simulators and financial advisors.
- With the two non-traditional investment strategies, we looked at real estate and business ownership.

So, we have discussed "investing wisely." But what about some practical examples? In the next chapter, we will discuss four practical case studies. But before we do, let's work through the following review and reflection questions:

Review Questions:
1. A. Which is more important with a savings account, having your money to make more money for you or to ensure you have a certain amount in the future?

B. How many months of living expenses should your emergency fund be able to cover?

C. What is an example of a big purchase?

2. A. Which is more critical with an investment, having your money to make more for you or to ensure you have a certain amount of money in the future?

B. Is it true that inflation eats away at the purchasing power of your money?

C. Is it true that your potential reward from an investment is all you have to consider when choosing an investment strategy?

D. Is it true that diversification urges you to spread your investments out over at least several investments?

E. What is considered the "eighth wonder of the world" by some financial enthusiasts?

3. A. What are the names of the 5 rather traditional investment strategies?

B. Can you really start investing with only $5?

C. What are the names of the two non-traditional investment strategies?

Reflection Questions:
1. If your monthly living expenses are $3,000/month, what is the minimum you should have in your emergency fund?

2. Given the impact of compounding interest, why should you start investing sooner rather than later?

3. How can ETFs be better than mutual funds for you?

4. How are you feeling about using real estate and/or business ownership as a part of your investment strategies? Explain.

5. Given all of this information, what are some key points in your action plan for investing wisely?

6. How are you doing with your "money mindset" work (knowledge, plan, and grit)?

Chapter 6. Four Case Studies

Remember from Chapter 1 that the four pillars of financial independence are: 1. Having a "money mindset," 2. Earning high, 3. Spending low, and 4. Investing wisely. We have discussed your money mindset (see Chapter 1), earning high (see Chapters 2 and 3), spending low (see Chapter 4), and investing wisely (see Chapter 5). In this chapter, we will look at the four case studies to help you think through how the material in this book relates to your goal of being financially independent.

Challenged But Made It

At Age 18. Meet Daniel. He was raised by a working-class single mother who lived paycheck to paycheck. His father was absent. He graduated from his public high school with a "B" average at the age of 18. He had no real career guidance or role models in financial independence.

Mindset. Through reading books like this one and listening to podcasts, he decided that he didn't have to be a victim of his circumstances. He set a goal to get a good job and make something of himself.

After High School. He saw an ad about becoming a truck driver. The company offered paid training and promised an income of at least $50,000/year. This was more than his mother ever made, even with her two jobs. He applied, was accepted, worked through the training, got his CDL license, and started his driving career.

As promised, he earned about $50,000/year in his first year, and by the end of his second year, he was making $55,000/year. During his second year, he set a goal of being financially independent by age 50 (i.e., stable income from his investments that exceeded his lifestyle needs).

Budgeting, Saving, and Investing. Because Daniel was sleeping in his truck or a hotel room, while on the road, and with his mother or cousin, when he was home, he did not have many bills to pay. In his first year, he aimed to save ½ of his money (i.e., $25,000). Daniel was able to do that, while also giving his mother $500/month to help out. In his second year, he saved over half his money (i.e., $30,000). By the time Daniel ended his third year of driving, he was making $60,000/year, had no debts, and saved $85,000, while giving his mother $500/month.

Daniel made sure he had 6 months of living expenses in his emergency fund. He invested in Exchange Traded Funds. He purchased a three family house and paid to get it fixed up. He lived in a small area, let his mother live in one unit, and rented the other unit out.

At Age 40. By the time he reached age 40 (i.e., 22 years of work), he was financially independent. He owned his truck and had two more trucks he leased out to other drivers. The three-family house was paid off, and he was still receiving rent from one of the units while he lived rent-free. He had money coming in from his ETF investments. He coaches other drivers from time to time for a little extra pocket money.

Key Points
- Despite Daniel's challenges, he worked on his mindset with books and podcasts.

- He got a job that had growth potential and low expenses (e.g., no student loans, low-cost housing, delayed getting a car).
- He made a budget that allowed him to save at least half of his money and build his emergency fund, while giving his mother $500/month.
- He invested in income-producing trucks, an income-producing house, and income-producing ETFs.
- He was financially independent at age 40 and still young enough to enjoy his life.
- Notice that he never went to college and had no student loan debt.

Good Start but Spent It All

At Age 18. Meet Emily. She grew up in a nurturing home where both parents were professionals. Her parents urged her to aspire to be something like a doctor or lawyer. In fact, her parents paid for her bachelor's degree, but Emily had to find ways to pay for her graduate work. Even though her family was well off financially, there was almost no talk about money. The big push was to have a professional career. She graduated from a private high school at 18 with a "B" average.

Mindset. Emily didn't give much thought to her mindset. She assumed that her parents were doing well, and she would follow in their footsteps. She believed she would retire somewhere around 60ish (i.e., around 60 years old) since her parents were still going strong at age 55.

After High School. Emily was accepted into one of her favorite colleges. Her parents paid for all of the expenses. She then got accepted into law school. She paid for law school with loans and a part-time job. She graduated from law school with $130,000 in student loans and received an entry-level job at a law firm, earning $60,000/year at age 26.

Budgeting, Saving, and Investing. Emily did not have a written budget. Even though she made $60,000/year, she had very little to show for it. She lived in an upscale apartment, leased a luxury car, was known for taking exotic trips, and ate out at least four times a week. She made the required payments on her student loan debts but did not budget for saving and investing.

Emily reasoned that she would "live a little" as her reward for so much hard work (i.e., earning a law degree and landing a job). She did not feel a need to have an emergency fund, because she made so much money, and she assumed her family would help, if needed. Her plan was to get serious about investing when she turned 30 years old.

At Age 40. When Emily reached age 40 (i.e., 14 years of work), she had a good job making $120,000/year. She was buying a $500,000 house and still owed $350,000 on the mortgage. She was still leasing luxury vehicles. Her student loan was paid off last year. She had $50,000 in her retirement account and $5,000 in her savings account. She has no idea what her firm has invested her $50,000 into, nor does she monitor her account. She no longer finds joy in being a lawyer, but she feels like she has to stay for the sake of her parents' expectations and the high income.

At the rate she is going, she will have to work until her 60s or become much more aggressive with lowering her expenses and increasing the amount she allocates to her investments. She will either have to get more involved in her investments or hire someone to help her get to where she wants to be in her 60s. At this point, she has spent a lot of money but has little wealth to show for it.

Key Points -

- Emily's nurturing family played a role in her not thinking she needed to work on her mindset. However, the ultimate responsibility belongs to Emily to work on her mindset.
- She went to college and law school to become a lawyer. She became a lawyer (many do not get a job in the field for which they went to college). However, in her first year as a lawyer, she had $130,000 in student loans and made only $60,000/year.
- Because she prioritized "living a little" over financial planning and discipline, she spent significant money that could have been saved and invested.
- After 14 years of working, she still does not have a significant emergency fund and has a long way to go to even be in the neighborhood of financial independence.

College Grad With Real Estate

At Age 18. Meet Alex. He was raised by working-class parents. He spent time going back and forth between his mother and father. Even though both parents loved him dearly and did a great job of staying active in his life, they were divorced for most of Alex's life. Alex graduated from high school at the age of 18.

Mindset. Alex knew he wanted more in life than simply living from paycheck to paycheck like his parents. After learning what they do and how much money they make, he decided to become an electrical engineer. His parents supported his decision and encouraged him to pursue his dreams, even though neither of them had gone to college. Alex also had teachers who urged him to pursue his dreams. His teachers also recommended that he read **Think and Grow Rich: A Black Choice** by Dennis Kimbro and Napoleon Hill. Alex read the books several times, made notes about the high points, and recited helpful affirmations to help him stay focused and disciplined. He knew he wanted to retire before 60 but did not have a written plan.

After High School. Alex was accepted into a college and earned his electrical engineering degree. Thanks to scholarships, financial aid, and his part time jobs, he graduated in five years with $15,000 in student loan debt. He landed an entry level electrical engineering job right out of college that paid $47,000/year at the age of 22.

Budgeting, Saving, and Investing. Alex worked on budgeting his money and following his budget. He drove modest used cars and lived in a one-bedroom apartment for his first two and a half years of working. This allowed him to build his six-month emergency fund, max out his company's 10% matching funds for retirement, and pay off his student loans.

Alex then focused on real estate. He purchased a four-unit apartment building by taking advantage of a first-time homebuyer's mortgage program, which offered favorable terms. After buying the property, Alex moved into one unit and rented out the other three (i.e., house hacking). He managed the property himself, learning the ropes of real estate management. He did most of the repair work, which minimized expenses. The rental income covered the mortgage and maintenance costs, while the surplus was used to accelerate the mortgage payoff and buy another four-unit apartment building. He repeated the cycle a total of five times.

At Age 40. By the time Alex turned 40 (i.e., 18 years of working), he had achieved financial independence. His 19 apartment units (i.e., remember he lived in one) covered all his living expenses and he had money growing in the retirement funds with his company.

Key Points

- Alex took responsibility for developing and maintaining his money mindset.
- He worked on keeping his college debt relatively low, by using scholarships, financial aid, and part-time jobs, while working towards a degree that positioned him for a profitable and in-demand career that he had aptitudes in.
- He made a budget and followed it to pay off his student loans, max out his company's retirement match, and build his emergency fund.
- He planned his work and worked his plan to build his real estate portfolio. He didn't know everything before he started. He learned and figured stuff out as he went.
- He was financially independent at age 40 and still young enough to enjoy his life.

The 40-Year Plan

At Age 18. Meet Jasmine. She grew up in a working class family with both father and mother living paycheck to paycheck. There was little talk in her family about financial planning. She graduated from her public high school with a "B" average.

Mindset. Jasmine knew she wanted more than simply living from paycheck to paycheck like her parents. She decided to go to college and pursue a degree in business administration, until she figured out what she wanted to do next. Jasmine hoped to get a good job after college and retire around 60-65. She heard some scriptures around her church like "I can do all things through Christ which strengthens me" (see Phil. 4:19; KJV). She would recite this scripture as her affirmation and mantra through college and her career.

After High School. Jasmine did two years at her local community college and then finished her bachelor's degree in business administration. Thanks to scholarships, financial aid, two years of college at the community college, and her part-time jobs, she graduated in five years with $12,000 in student loan debt. She landed an entry-level job as a management trainee right out of college that paid $40,000/year with an excellent benefit package at the age of 22.

Budgeting, Saving, and Investing. Starting with her first paycheck, Jasmine developed and followed a written budget. After accounting for her necessities, she made sure to allocate money for her company's retirement matching funds. She lived in a modest efficiency apartment and drove a used four-cylinder car. After three years, she was proud of having paid off her student loans and built her six-month emergency fund. Her salary had grown to $46,000.

Jasmine's investment strategy was to max out her company's 401(k) contributions (i.e., $23,000/year) and then start buying a house. She planned to use any extra money to pay off the house as soon as possible and then start investing in ETFs in her Roth retirement account outside of her company's retirement program.

At Age 40. After 17 years of work, Jasmine not only had her emergency fund, but she also had over $600,000 in her retirement fund. She paid off her house last year. Jasmine buys used cars that are five years old and drives them until they die on her. She is not financially independent, but she is doing very well for herself. She should be financially independent by her 50th birthday.

Key Points –
- Jasmine took responsibility for her mindset.
- Jasmine went to college to get a "good job." She stayed focused and disciplined enough to finish college and get a job. She also kept her debt low enough to quickly pay it off.
- She did an excellent job of getting her emergency fund together and maxing out her retirement account.
- Jasmine took a conservative route, but it worked out for her. There is no one-size-fits-all.

As We Close This Chapter ...

In this chapter, we have looked at four teenagers who made decisions and took actions that led to different outcomes. The next chapter discusses building your customized action plan for financial independence. But before we do, let's work through the following reflection questions:

Reflection Questions
1. What are some things you like about Daniel's story (i.e., Challenged but Made It) that may be able to help you with your financial independence? What are some things you wish you could have given him some advice on to make his journey smoother?

2. What are some things you like about Emily's story (i.e., Good Start but Spent it All) that may be able to help you with your financial independence? What are some things you wish you could have given her some advice on to make her journey smoother?

3. What are some things you like about Alex's story (i.e., College Grad with Real Estate) that may be able to help you with your financial independence? What are some things you wish you could have given him some advice on to make his journey smoother?

4. What are some things you like about Jasmine's story (i.e., The 40-Year Plan) that may be able to help you with your financial independence? What are some things you wish you could have given her some advice on to make her journey smoother?

Chapter 7. Your Action Plan for Financial Independence

Imagine two teenagers. The first has dreams of being financially independent and living a great life. He wants to be some kind of engineer, and he reasons that he will figure things out as he goes. The second not only has a dream of being financially independent, but she also has an action plan that includes learning more about material outlined in this book and practicing the discipline needed to carry out the action plan. Which teenager do you think is more likely to achieve financial independence? I hope you said the second one.

Remember from chapter 1 that the four pillars of financial independence are 1. Having a "money mindset," 2. Earning high, 3. Spending low, and 4. Investing wisely. We have discussed your "money mindset" (see Chapter 1), earning high (see Chapters 2 and 3), spending low (see Chapter 4), and investing wisely (see Chapter 5). In the last chapter, we discussed some case studies to help you think through how the material in this book relates to your life. In this chapter, we finally pull the pieces together and build your action plan for financial independence.

5 Key Elements of Your Action Plan

Different people may have different elements to their action plan. The following are five key areas that I recommend you focus on in developing your action plan for financial independence:

101

1. Your WHY Statement. Think about a bow and arrow. The further you pull the arrow back on the string, the further forward it will go when released. This is similar to the power of your WHY. The stronger your why, the further you will go with carrying out your action plan.

Take some time to answer the following questions:
- How would you feel if you were financially independent by age 40? Why?
- How would your close loved ones feel? Why?
- If God is important to you, how do you think God will feel? Why?
- Who would you like to help? How? Why?
- How would your "haters" feel? Why?

Take your answers and craft your compelling WHY statement. Here is a prompt, "The following are some of my top reasons WHY I keep taking action towards my financial independence:
1. ...
2. ...
3. ..."

2. Inspiration Material. Inspiration is about helping you *feel* like carrying out your action plan. Inspirational quotes, affirmations, a vision board, and listening material can help.

What are some *quotes* that inspire you or make you feel like *taking action*? Make a list of at least five. Christians may find the following passages of scriptures helpful:
- "I can do all this through him who gives me strength." Philippians 4:13; NIV
- "No, in all these things we are more than conquerors through him who loved us." Romans 8:37; NIV

- "... because the one who is in you is greater than the one who is in the world." I John 4:4b; NIV
Search "empowering quotes for financial independence."

What are some *affirmations* that inspire you or make you feel like *taking action*? An affirmation, as used here, is what you declare to be true for you to help you take action. Make a list of at least five. The following are some examples:

- If it is going to be, it is up to me. No one is coming to my rescue. I am responsible for my consistent strategic action.
- I can make a 1,000 mile journey, if I keep moving in the right direction. I'm going to keep moving today!
- I climb mountains, endure storms, and solve problems. I'm not a helpless victim.
- No matter how I feel, I will keep moving in the right direction.
- Yesterday is over. Today is a new day, and I am moving in the right direction.
- I can learn whatever I need to learn.
- My faith is stronger than my fears and doubts.
- My past doesn't define me; my mindset and actions do.
- My environment doesn't define me; my mindset and actions do.

Search "empowering affirmations for financial independence."

A *vision board* is where you cut out some pictures of what you want and *what you will do* to get what you want and affix the images to a piece of cardboard or something to be displayed on a wall to inspire you. Think about what you want, your goals, and *what you must do to get there*. Look through some magazines or search for keywords and look at the images. Copy and paste what inspires you on a vision board. Study the article, "How to Create a Vision Board"^{xliv} for more information.

Your *listening material* can be podcasts, audiobooks, music, and the like. The idea is to keep something positive and constructive on your mind that helps you *consistently take strategic action,* instead of allowing your mind to waddle in negativity and distractions.

3. SMART Goals. SMART is an acronym where the S stands for specific, M for measurable, A for attainable, R for relevant, and T for time bound. Consider the following three examples. Which ones are more like SMART goals?

A. I want to make $100,000/year by the time I reach age 30.
B. I want to make a lot of money.

C. I want to have a nice car after I graduate from college.
D. When I graduate from college in six years, I want to purchase a three-year-old Toyota Camry.

E. I want to draw $50,000/year from my $500,000 portfolio of investments, by the time I'm 30 years old.
F. I want to be rich by age 30.

Hopefully, you chose A, D, and E. The challenge of B, C, and F is they are too vague to be measured for success.

4. Accountability. As used here, accountability means telling someone how you are doing with what you said you would do. The "someone" can be yourself and others. The following are four helpful ways of being accountable for carrying out your action plan:

1. Journaling. If you have to choose between some fancy computer or phone app that you will stop using when there is an update that you don't like or an old-fashioned pen and notebook, I personally like the pen and notebook or a simple document on my phone or computer. Do what works for you *consistently*.

The following are some prompts and/or questions to help you with your journaling:

- On a scale of 1 to 5, with 5 being excellent, how well have I carried out my action plan since my last entry?
- What can and should I do to improve my grade or hold on to a 5 out of 5?
- What has been a "win" for me this week? Explain. What am I going to do about this? Report on this in your next entry.
- What has been my greatest challenge since the last entry? Explain. What am I going to do about this? Report on this in your next entry.
- Who do I need to talk to regarding my questions, concerns, for accountability, and/or for inspiration? What is my plan for talking with them? Report on this in your next entry.
- What else do I want to make note of?

Study the article "How to Set and Achieve Goals with Journaling"[xlv] for more information.

2. Mentor. As used here, a mentor is someone you respect as being more accomplished than you, you trust them to help you be accountable for carrying out your action plan, and they consent to giving you helpful encouragement. You all can meet weekly or monthly to start and then monthly or quarterly after there is some momentum. Your parents, teachers, and Pastor may be able to give you some suggestions.

3. Accountability Partner. As used here, an accountability partner is someone you consider to be your peer. You both are working on carrying out action plans for financial independence. You all may talk weekly about your "wins" and how to respond to challenges in carrying out your action plans. After you all develop momentum, you may send written updates bi-weekly and talk bi-weekly as needed. Schoolmates, friends, relatives, etc., especially those willing to read and work through this book with you would be good prospects for being an accountability partner. Study the article, "Accountability Partners: Don't Achieve Your Goals Alone!"[xlvi] for more information.

4. Accountability Group. As used here, an accountability group is a group of 3 to 12 people who are your peers. You all are working on carrying out action plans for financial independence. You all may meet monthly and share with one another about your "wins" and how to respond to challenges in carrying out your action plans. Schoolmates, friends, relatives, etc., especially those who are willing to read and work through this book with you, would be good prospects for being in this group. Study the article, "Accountability Groups: The Support You Need To Succeed"[xlvii] [iv] for more information.

5. Consistent Strategic Action. Goals are essential, but they are simply words, if you don't take consistent strategic action. You should aim to take daily, weekly, and monthly actions (i.e., consistent) aimed at achieving your goals (i.e., strategic).

Throughout this book, we've discussed the four pillars of financial independence: 1. Having a "money mindset," 2. Earning high, 3. Spending low, and 4. Investing wisely. The following are some examples of consistent strategic actions you can take in each area:

Having a "Money Mindset"

Daily –

- Read at least 5 pages of a great book on personal development (i.e., books about how to build your confidence, how to stay disciplined, how to break free from toxic thinking and environments, etc.).
- Read at least 5 pages of a great book on personal finances (i.e., books about occupational trends, profitable side hustles, how to invest in the stock market, how to invest in real estate, etc.).
- Develop and read your "Money Mindset" document. This is a living document (i.e., you will be adding to it and modifying it over time) that includes notes about your WHY statement (see above), inspirational material (i.e., helps you *feel like taking consistent strategic action*; inspirational quotes, affirmations, etc.), and reminders about the pillars of financial independence (see below). This can be a great place to add something like a vision board also.
- Listen to inspirational material like podcasts, audiobooks, music, etc.

Weekly –

- Summarize your reading for the week. Making summary notes of your reading will help you remember the material and provide a quicker way to review the material than re-reading the entire book.
- Make a journal entry. Do what works for you, but it may be helpful to note whether you are consistent with your daily actions, whether you carried out the actions that you said you would last week, what were some good things that happened to/for you this week, what new information have you learned, what has been challenging, what actions will you take this week, etc.

- Talk to your accountability partner about your consistency and any questions you may have. Of course you need to find an accountability partner. This may simply be someone who joins you in reading this book, developing an action plan, and carrying out their plan. Make sure this person will help you move forward with your plan, instead of pull you backwards or distract you. If you cannot find anyone positive, look until you find one. Having no accountability partner can be better than having a lousy accountability partner.
- Talk to at least one person who can help you in your pursuit of financial independence. This can be someone doing the job you are thinking about, someone who owns a business you are thinking about starting, someone who seems to be doing well with their budgeting or mindset, someone who has skills you would like to develop, etc. You may need to talk to someone who can introduce you to someone else who you want to talk to. You may want to talk with a peer about how they are coming with their action plan. You can also ask people what books, podcasts, resources, etc. they recommend.

Monthly –
- Talk with a mentor about your consistency and any questions you have. Of course, you need to find a mentor. You may want to start with your parents, a successful relative, a teacher, someone in your church, a business owner, etc. They may not want to be your "mentor," but they may be willing to talk with you from time to time.
- Talk to your accountability group about your consistency and any questions you have. Of course, you need to find an accountability group. This may simply be a group of teens who join you in reading this book, developing action plans, and carrying out their

plans. You may need to start such a group. See *"8 Tips for Starting and Maintaining an Accountability Group"* in the Appendix.

Earning High

Daily –
- Add to your "Money Mindset" document and read daily reminders and affirmations that remind you of things like you can learn whatever you need to learn, you are proactive and have grit (focus and discipline), you can make a 1,000 mile journey, if you keep moving in the right direction (i.e., the power of consistent strategic action), etc.
- Add and read reminders of how what you are doing today relates to you getting to a place of earning high. For example, you may be completing high school, exploring career opportunities, participating in sports for the sake of scholarship opportunities, etc.
- Carry out your "money mindset" actions. If you don't keep your mindset strong, you cannot do anything else. Consistently earning high, spending low, and investing wisely calls for you to maintain your "money mindset."

Weekly –
- Add to your journal entry any notes about what you have learned this week about you and/or your quest to earn high. See comments about weekly journaling under money mindset above.
- Talk to your accountability partner about your consistency and any questions you have. See comments about accountability partners under money mindset above.
- Talk to at least one person who can help you in your pursuit of financial independence. See comments about

talking to someone weekly under money mindset above.

Monthly –
- Talk with a mentor about your consistency and any questions you have. See comments about mentoring under money mindset above.
- Talk to your accountability group about your consistency and any questions you have. See comments about accountability groups under money mindset above.

Spending Low

Daily –
- Add to your "Money Mindset" document and read daily reminders and affirmations that remind you of things like your long term financial independence is more important than impressing your broke peers, your current condition is not your final destination, better days are coming, etc. Remember that you are not your stuff. If you are a loser, wearing expensive clothes will not make you a winner. You are a loser wearing expensive clothes. See yourself as a winner who is simply in a money saving season.
- Add and read reminders of how what you are doing today relates to what you are doing today relates to your journey to financial independence. For example, you may be walking or riding a bike to save money, bringing your lunch, not buying new clothes, etc., so you will have money for your training program, application fees, etc.
- Carry out your "money mindset" actions. If you don't keep your mindset strong, you cannot do anything else. Consistently earning high, spending low, and investing wisely calls for you to maintain your "money mindset."

Weekly –

- Add to your journal entry any notes about what you have learned this week about you and/or your quest to spend low. See comments about weekly journaling under money mindset above.
- Talk to your accountability partner about your consistency and any questions you have. See comments about accountability partners under money mindset above.
- Talk to at least one person who can help you in your pursuit of financial independence. This can be someone who has a great mindset even though they don't seem to be spending a lot of money, someone who can help you save money with your living expenses, help you with an expected big purchase, etc. See comments about talking to someone weekly under money mindset above.

Monthly –

- Talk with a mentor about your consistency and any questions you have. See comments about mentoring under money mindset above.
- Talk to your accountability group about your consistency and any questions you have. See comments about accountability groups under money mindset above.

Investing Wisely

Daily –

- Add to your "Money Mindset" document and read daily reminders and affirmations that remind you of things like the power of compounding interest and how consistent strategic action will help you reach financial independence, if you keep going.

- Carry out your "money mindset" actions. If you don't keep your mindset strong, you cannot do anything else. Consistently earning high, spending low, and investing wisely calls for you to maintain your "money mindset."
- Set up something like your Acorn account so that your pocket change is invested in something like the SCHG Exchange Traded Fund (i.e., large cap growth stocks like Apple, Microsoft, Amazon, etc.).

Weekly –
- Add to your journal entry any notes about what you have learned this week about you and/or your quest to invest wisely. See comments about weekly journaling under money mindset above.
- Talk to your accountability partner about your consistency and any questions you have. See comments about accountability partners under money mindset above.
- Talk to at least one person who can help you in your pursuit of financial independence. This can be someone known for investing in the stock market, a real estate investor, a business owner, has a great mindset, etc. See comments about talking to someone weekly under money mindset above.

Monthly –
- Talk with a mentor about your consistency and any questions you have. See comments about mentoring under money mindset above.
- Talk to your accountability group about your consistency and any questions you have. See comments about accountability groups under money mindset above.

Your Customized Action Plan

Alright, we have covered a lot of material in this book and this chapter. The following questions are designed to help you develop your customized action plan for financial independence. Please seriously consider the following questions and record your answers either with pen and paper or digitally. If you get stuck on one of the questions move on to the next one and come back to the one you got stuck on. We will talk about how to structure your answers later.

1. Since mindset is so important, what are two personal development books you want to focus on? What are two personal finance books you want to focus on? What are some helpful affirmations for you? Who are some people you plan to talk to about being your mentor? Who are some people you plan to talk to about being your accountability partner? What are your plans regarding an accountability group?

- Personal Development
- Personal Finances
- Affirmations
- Mentors
- Accountability Partners
- Accountability Group

2. Given what you know today, what are your SMART goals in the four pillars of financial independence (mindset, earning, spending, and investing) for 10 years from now, 1 year from now, and 90 days from now?

Money Mindset
- 10 years
- 5 years

- 1 year
- 90 days

Earn High
- 10 years
- 5 years
- 1 year
- 90 days

Spend Low
- 10 years
- 5 years
- 1 year
- 90 days

Invest Wisely
- 10 years
- 5 years
- 1 year
- 90 days

3. What consistent strategic actions do you plan to take in the four pillars of financial independence (mindset, earning, spending, and investing; daily, weekly, and monthly)?

Money Mindset
- Daily
- Weekly
- Monthly

Earn High
- Daily
- Weekly
- Monthly

Spend Low
- Daily
- Weekly
- Monthly

Invest Wisely
- Daily
- Weekly
- Monthly

4. Does your response to question #3 have enough accountability built into it (i.e., journal, mentor, accountability partner, and accountability group)?

The Structure of Your Action Plan

I recommend that you do what works for you. You may want to consider the following structure:

[Your name] 's Action Plan Overview for
Financial Independence
(as of [date])

List a summary of your WHY with some inspiring material to help you keep going, especially when you don't feel like it.

List one compelling 90-day goal in each of the four pillar areas (i.e., money mindset, earn high, spend low, and invest wisely)

List a summary of your daily, weekly, and monthly actions for each goal.

All of the above should fit on one page and be posted somewhere you can see it regularly like the bathroom, your nightstand, under your pillow, etc. Attached to this overview, you can add your other goals, plans, inspirational material, etc.

Again, do what works for you. If what you are doing is helping you take consistent strategic action, it is working. If you are not taking consistent strategic action, something is not working.

As We Close This Chapter ...

In this chapter, we have discussed the following:
- Your WHY statement. How will your financial independence make you and your significant others feel?
- Inspirational material. We talked about inspiring quotes, affirmations, a vision board, and listening material.
- SMART goals. We discussed goals being specific, measurable, attainable, relevant, and time bound.
- Consistent strategic action. I gave you practical examples of daily, weekly, and monthly actions you can take towards your financial independence.
- Accountability. We talked about journaling, mentors, accountability partners, and accountability groups
- Your customized action plan. I gave you guidance on developing the contents of your plan and the structure of the document.

We are about to conclude this book. But before we do that, let's work through the following review and reflection questions:

Review Questions:
1. A. How many parts of your action plan did we discuss above?

B. Was accountability one of the parts?

2. A. Were you given information on journaling and accountability partners?

B. Were the examples of actions you can take on a daily, weekly, and monthly basis in the four pillar areas of financial independence supposed to be the only things that you can do?

3. A. Your mindset is not really important. True or False

B. If you don't follow the suggestions about the structure of your action plan, you are doing it wrong. True or False

Reflection Questions:
1. Do you believe that the information in this book can help you reach financial independence, if you study and apply the material? Explain.

2. Do you believe that you are able to understand and apply the material in this book, especially the development of your action plan? Explain.

3. Will you take the challenge of this book to plan your work and work your plan to be the first (or one of the next) financially independent person in your family and community? Explain.

Conclusion

Congratulations on making it to the conclusion of this book. Most people don't finish reading their books. I pray that you have not only read this book but that you have understood the material, developed an action plan, and are committed to YOUR FINANCIAL INDEPENDENCE. You may live to be 80+ years old. You cannot count on big businesses to give you a pension or big government to support you with Social Security. You must take responsibility for yourself. You have to start now because you can use the power of compounding interest to your advantage more than if you wait until age 30, 40, or 50.

If you started investing $200/month at age 20 until age 60 at a 10% annual return, you would have about $1,118,000. If you wait until age 30 and started investing $200/month at 10% annual return, you would have about $415,000. If you wait until age 40, you would only have about $144,000. And if you wait until age 50, you would only have about $40,000.

If you started investing $200/month at age 20 until age 30, you would have about $40,000. If you left the money alone, it would grow to about $697,000 by the time you reach age 60. If you invested $1,400/month from age 20-40 at a 10% annual return, you would have about $1,000,000 at age 40. I hope you can see the power of starting early and the challenges you will face if you start later.

You should feel a certain amount of satisfaction about reading this entire book. You are familiar with concepts and practical tips related to having a "money mindset," earning high, spending low, and investing wisely.

However, you must "plan your work and work your plan" to be financially independent. Remember Daniel, Alex, and Jasmine from Chapter 6. They did more than read a book. They made their plans and followed them.

You can be the first (or next) millionaire in your family. You can help other people in your community with your donations and your example of tuning your thoughts into actions that lead to financial independence. *And that is what I pray you will do.*

Let me ask one last time ...

.... If you could help a teenager, in 60 seconds and at no cost to you, would you?

This book, **Money Management for Teens**, can help so many teenagers, if I can simply get the book into their hands.

Research shows that before a person looks inside the book, they look at the cover and number of reviews. I need you to leave a review so that when others consider this book, they will see a high number of reviews. You can leave a review in 60 seconds and at no cost to you.

Your review can help teenagers see that no matter where they are now, they can take control of their lives and be the first (or next) financially independent person in their family.

Your review can help a teenager see that even though college may not be for them, financial independence can still be in their future.

Your review can help a parent or caregiver purchase this book for teenagers in their lives.

All you have to do is scan the QR code below to leave your review:

Thank YOU so much.

Fun fact: If you provide something of value to another person, it makes you more valuable to them. If you believe this book will help a teenager, send them a copy.

Appendix

For Further Study

The following are some of the best books for you to study as you pursue your financial independence. As much as you may want to simply study books of money management, I strongly recommend that you study some mindset and personal development books as well. If you don't work on your mindset and personal development, it will be almost impossible for you to achieve financial independence, and if you do, you probably will not enjoy it.

Mindset and Personal Development

Think and Grow Rich: A Black Choice by Dennis Kimbro and Napoleon Hill. This is a culturally enriched adaptation of Napoleon Hill's classic, **Think and Grow Rich**. This version focuses on empowering African Americans, by sharing success stories of Black entrepreneurs and leaders. You will be encouraged to harness your potential, overcome obstacles, and achieve financial success.

The Seven Habits of Highly Effective People by Stephen Covey. This book outlines seven habits that are essential for personal and professional effectiveness. You will learn about 1. Being proactive, 2. Beginning with the end in mind, 3. Putting first things first, 4. Thinking win-win, 5. Seeking to understand and then to be understood, 6. Synergy, and 7. Sharpening the saw.

The Psychology of Money by Morgan Housel. This book discusses the complex relationship between money and human behavior. Financial success is more about how we think and act than about intelligence or knowledge. You will be encouraged to understand your thought process and make better financial decisions.

Mindset by Carol S. Dweck. This book does a great job of explaining the concepts of "fixed" vs. "growth" mindsets. You will be encouraged to develop a growth mindset that can adapt to the challenges and opportunities you are sure to encounter in your life.

Grit by Angela Duckworth. This book is about having passion and perseverance for long-term goals (i.e., grit). Those with grit can work through adversities and accomplish their goals. Thankfully, you can develop your grit, even if it doesn't come naturally for you.

Atomic Habits by James Clear explores how small and incremental changes in behavior can lead to significant improvements over time. The book gives you practical strategies for building good habits, breaking bad ones, and mastering the tiny actions that lead to lasting change.

Money Management

Rich Dad Poor Dad by Robert Kiyosaki. This book discusses how getting a good education and a good job is not always the best way to financial independence. You will be urged to look carefully at your financial education, investing, and entrepreneurship.

I Will Teach You to Be Rich by Ramit Sethi. This book gives practical guidance on automating your finances towards investing early and spending on what truly matters to you. You will learn about budgeting, saving, and investing.

The Little Book of Common Sense Investing by John C. Bogle. This book discusses how buying and holding low-cost index funds to match market performance rather than trying to beat it is the way to go. You will learn that most "expert fund managers" and stock pickers are too expensive and unreliable when compared to simply investing in ETFs.

The Richest Man in Babylon by George S. Clason. This book presents excellent financial lessons through a series of parables. You will learn about building your wealth by way of proportionate saving, investing wisely, and seeking wise counsel.

Answers to the Review Questions

Chapter 1. "Money Mindset"
1. A. Approximately 78% of U.S. workers.
B. About $37,684
C. 67 years old and $200,000
D. About $1,907/month

2. A. investments, expenses
B. comfortably, travel, and help
C. $1,000,000, $1,000,000, $100,000
D. Money, Earning, Spending, and Investing

3. A. financial, action, execute
B. believe, learn, plan, work, support system, mind, challenges

4. A. five people
B. limit, eliminate, positive

Chapter 2. As a Teenager, "Should You Focus on Making Money or Going to School"?
1. A. *Positives - Higher earning potential and broader career opportunities. Negatives - High cost and debt and time commitment.*
B. Yes, Yes
C. True
D. True
E. True

2. job, gigs, side hustle

Chapter 3. Earning High
1. A. aptitude, money, demand

B. True
C. False

2. A. 7
B. No
C. False

3. A. 7
B. No
C. Yes

Chapter 4. Spending Low
1. A. Money mindset, earn high, spend low, and invest wisely.
B. Spender, saver, investor, and giver; No

2. A. 7
B. Fear of missing out
C. They are used to pay for the services the government provides to the citizens like road, law enforcement, social security, the military, etc.
D. The "snowball" approach

3. A. income, expenses
B. 70% of your income is to pay for your living expenses. 20% is used for paying off debt, saving, and investing. And 10% is given to something like your church, charity, or the like.
C. expenses, income

4. A. 12
B. No
C. False

5. False

Chapter 5. Investing Wisely
1. A. Ensure you have a certain amount in the future.
B. 3- 6 months
C. A car, an apartment, a computer

2. A. Having your money to make money for you.
B. Yes
C. No
D. Yes
E. Compounding interest

3. A. Bonds, stocks, cryptocurrency, mutual funds, and exchanged traded funds
B. Yes
C. Real estate and business ownership

Chapter 6. Four Case Studies
No review questions

Chapter 7. Your Action Plan for Financial Independence
1. A. 5
B. Yes

2. A. Yes
B. No

3. A. False
B. False

8 Tips for Starting and Maintaining an Accountability Group

As noted in several places in this book, an accountability group can help you stay focused on carrying out your action plan. Here are 8 tips for starting and maintaining an accountability group:

1. Keep the Group's Mission Front and Center. Develop a mission statement and have members agree to support it. The mission statement may be something like "The mission of this group is to help its members develop and carry out their action plans for financial independence." Recite the mission statement at each session. At least quarterly have the group to discuss how it is being true to its mission and how it can improve in carrying out its mission.

2. Work on Having Only Members Who Support the Group's Mission. Group members may sign a covenant to support the group's mission and recite it during each session with the group. Group members may be required to give some version of their action plan to the group and give feedback on the action plans of others in the group.

No one should be allowed to be disrespectful to anyone in the group. And no one should be allowed to regularly break the rules of the group, including the rule to contribute to constructive discussions about the groups' agenda. It is good to invite and try to bring the right people to the group. And it is important to keep the wrong people from distracting or disturbing the group.

3. Develop and Follow an Agenda. The following are some ideas to consider:

- Developing and reciting some kind of covenant that includes the group's mission would be recommended.
- Have the group members to share their joys and concerns since the last session.
- Discuss and agree on issues that require the group's input.
- And have some kind of presentation for each session. For example, you all should work through this book as a group. And you can work through the recommended books as well. You can invite special guest to discuss various topics and have a question and answer session afterwards (see tip #8).

4. Set a Regular Meeting Time. The group sessions may be monthly or whatever works for the group. The sessions may be about 60-90 minutes. Establishing a set time is recommended or at least schedule out your next 6-9 sessions, so group members can plan accordingly.

5. Create a Safe and Supportive Environment. Work on having a non-judgmental space where members feel comfortable sharing their financial situations and challenges. Encourage open dialogue about financial challenges, successes, and learning experiences. Open communication builds trust and allows members to learn from each other's experiences.

6. Promote Accountability Partners. Urge members to pair up with one another for accountability and one-on-one support between meetings. These partnerships help keep individuals motivated and accountable for their progress. Be prepared to help especially some of the shy people to find at least a temporary accountability partner.

7. Celebrate Milestones. Recognizing and celebrating small victories, like reaching a savings goal, keeps morale high and encourages continued effort. This positive reinforcement helps maintain long-term commitment to financial goals.

8. Invite Guest Speakers or Mentors. Bringing in financial experts or older peers who have achieved financial independence can provide valuable insights and inspiration. These guests can offer new perspectives and inspire members to stay on track.

Biblical Principles Regarding Money Management

Even though I am an ordained minister of the Gospel, I didn't want to make this a book of sermons. This book is written to be a practical guide for teenagers to plan their work and work their plan to be financially independent.

However, I want Christian teenagers and churches to know that there are biblical principles to support the material found in this book. Read the following passages of scripture in the New International Version of the Bible: Matthew 16:26; 1 Timothy 6:17-19; Luke 19:13, 16-20, 22-23; Ecclesiastes 11:2; 4:12

Commentary

Matthew 16:26 supports the idea that if you have to choose between the riches of this world or your soul, your soul is more important. However, in many cases, we are not confronted with an either or situation. Often, we can choose both and. We can have a saved soul and financial well-being.

I Timothy 6:17-19 supports the idea that rich Christians should put their hope in God, not in their uncertain riches. The riches of today can be gone tomorrow. God provides His people with blessings for them to enjoy. Rich Christians are to be known for being rich in good deeds. Good deeds can include giving money, but many people need education and coaching to be wise financial stewards. And there needs to be advocacy to make sure the systems (e.g., educational system, economic system, criminal justice system, social work system, etc.) gives especially the less fortunate a chance to get on their feet. There are blessings for the rich Christians who are rich in good deeds.

Luke 19:13, 16-20, 22-23 supports the idea that God wants His people to be profitable with what He has invested in them. The more profitable we are, the more God is subject to bless us. There is a such thing as God being angry with our poor and wicked stewardship and even punishing us for such. Many financial troubles are a product of an unfair systems (e.g., poor education, lack of exposure to opportunities, discrimination, etc.). But there are also many financial troubles that come from poor stewardship by the individual (e.g., not having a "money management mindset," not earning high, spending too much on consumer items, not giving oneself to learning about investing and actually investing, etc.). Being a profitable steward of our finances is as spiritual as praying, worshiping, and Bible study.

Ecclesiastes 11:2 supports the idea of diversifying one's investments. All investments look good in the beginning, but many run into unforeseen problems. By having several investments, if one falls off, you still have a chance for some of the others to be profitable.

Ecclesiastes 4:12 supports the idea of aiming to have a supportive accountability partner or two. More than two people is the definition of an accountability group. Three focused and determined teenagers can provide great support to one another in pursuing their financial independence.

About the Author

Robert E. Baines, Jr. served 29 years as a Pastor. During that period, he served two churches in the state of New York and two churches in the state of Ohio. As a Pastor, he has ministered to people who have experienced an array of financial challenges and victories.

In addition to his Pastoral experience, he holds a number of degrees, the highest of which is a Doctor of Ministry degree with a focus on economic and spiritual empowerment.

By the grace of God, he and his wife are doing well financially. However, he has serious concerns about the millennials and younger generations' ability to obtain financial independence. Even though these generations have the benefit of technologies that could only be dreamed of 40-50 years ago, they don't seem to have the financial literacy or financial discipline needed to live in a society that cannot count on pensions from big corporations or Social Security from the federal government.

His prayer is that this book will be a guide for his young grandchildren (ages 10, 8, and 5 at the time of this writing) as well as teenagers around the United States and even the world.

Other Books by the Author

The following are some other books that Dr. Baines has published on Amazon:

How To Live Your Best Life: A Guide for Discovering and Living by What Matters Most to You, Instead of Just Surviving

How To Stay Focused: A Guide for Doing What Really Matters Most, In Spite of Distractions

Dealing With Difficult People: 31 Empowering Christian Devotionals For Those Dealing With Negative, Manipulative, or Mean People (Dealing With Difficult People Series, Volume 4)

End Notes

[i] Forbes Advisor. (2024). Living paycheck to paycheck statistics. Retrieved from https://www.forbes.com/advisor/banking/living-paycheck-to-paycheck-statistics-2024/

[ii] PYMNTS. (2024). Nearly half of US consumers earning $100K live paycheck to paycheck. Retrieved from https://www.pymnts.com/consumer-finance/2024/nearly-half-of-us-consumers-earning-100k-live-paycheck-to-paycheck/

[iii] Wikipedia. (n.d.). Per capita personal income in the United States. Retrieved from https://bit.ly/PerCapitaUS

[iv] Visual Capitalist. (n.d.). America's average retirement savings by age. Retrieved from https://www.visualcapitalist.com/americas-average-retirement-savings-by-age/

[v] Social Security Administration. (n.d.). Social Security FAQs. Retrieved from https://faq.ssa.gov/en-us/Topic/article/KA-01903

[vi] These numbers were calculated by the use the Bishinews Financial Calculators at Bishinews Financial Calculators. (n.d.). Financial Calculators. Retrieved from https://play.google.com/store/apps/details?id=com.financial.calculator&hl=en_US

[vii] U.S. Chamber of Commerce. (n.d.). Mos Bows founder Moziah Bridges. Retrieved from https://www.uschamber.com/co/good-company/growth-studio/mos-bows-founder-moziah-bridges

[viii] Caribbean Life. (n.d.). Leanna Archer. Retrieved from https://www.caribbeanlife.com/leanna-archer

[ix] Web.com. (n.d.). The SuperJam story: Multimillion success. Retrieved from https://www.web.com/blog/superjam-story-multimillion-success/

[x] Forbes. (2008). Teen millionaires. Retrieved from https://www.forbes.com/2008/02/09/teen-millionaires-startups-ent-cook-cx-ml_0211cook.html

[xi] Wikipedia. (n.d.). Nick D'Aloisio. Retrieved from https://en.wikipedia.org/wiki/Nick_D'Aloisio

[xii] Mind. (n.d.). Confidence and self-esteem. Retrieved from https://www.mind.org.uk/for-young-people/feelings-and-experiences/confidence-and-self-esteem/

[xiii] Paradigm Treatment. (n.d.). Build and maintain a strong support system. Retrieved from https://paradigmtreatment.com/build-maintain-strong-support-system/

[xiv] Slow Chat Health. (2019). Journaling perks. Retrieved from https://slowchathealth.com/2019/10/04/journaling-perks/

[xv] Indeed. (n.d.). Where to find a job. Retrieved from https://www.indeed.com/career-advice/finding-a-job/where-to-find-a-job

[xvi] We Think Twice. (n.d.). Interview tips for teens. Retrieved from https://www.wethinktwice.acf.hhs.gov/interview-tips-teens

[xvii] Las Vegas-Clark County Library District. (n.d.). Basic information on how to link an app. Retrieved from https://lvccld.org/wp-content/uploads/sites/54/2021/06/TW_Basic-Info-Link-App_030819.pdf

[xviii] MyDoh. (n.d.). How to make a resume for teens with examples. Retrieved from https://www.mydoh.ca/learn/blog/career/how-to-make-a-resume-for-teens-with-examples/

[xix] Greenlight. (n.d.). Online jobs for teens. Retrieved from https://greenlight.com/learning-center/earning/online-jobs-for-teens

[xx] Medium. (2024). The best skills to learn as a teen in 2024. Retrieved from https://medium.com/practice-in-public/the-best-skills-to-learn-as-a-teen-in-2024-a6c98c6be23f

[xxi] Experience Life. (n.d.). The living experiment: Satisfaction vs. success. Retrieved from https://experiencelife.lifetime.life/article/the-living-experiment-satisfaction-vs-success/

[xxii] Youth.gov. (n.d.). Career exploration and skill development. Retrieved from https://bit.ly/CareerExplorationandSkillDevelopment

[xxiii] SAS Blogs. (2015). Helping your teens with career self-discovery. Retrieved from https://blogs.sas.com/content/efs/2015/05/28/helping-your-teens-with-career-self-discovery/

[xxiv] EducationPlanner. (n.d.). Self-assessments. Retrieved from http://www.educationplanner.org/students/self-assessments

[xxv] American Hospital Association. (2024). 4 takeaways on coming shift in health services demand. Retrieved from https://www.aha.org/aha-center-health-innovation-market-scan/2024-07-02-4-takeaways-coming-shift-health-services-demand
- Peter G. Peterson Foundation. (2024). Why are Americans paying more for healthcare? Retrieved from https://www.pgpf.org/blog/2024/01/why-are-americans-paying-more-for-healthcare
- HealthManagement.org. (2024). Adapting the future of healthcare to an ageing population. Retrieved from https://healthmanagement.org/c/hospital/News/adapting-the-future-of-healthcare-to-an-ageing-population

[xxvi] U.S. Bureau of Labor Statistics. (2015). Overview of projections to 2024. Retrieved from https://www.bls.gov/opub/mlr/2015/article/overview-of-projections-to-2024.htm

[xxvii] Danaher. (2024). Job market trends 2024. Retrieved from https://jobsblog.danaher.com/blog/job-market-trends-2024/
- McLane Middleton. (2024). Employment law trends every employer should be aware of for 2024. Retrieved from https://www.mclane.com/insights/employment-law-trends-every-employer-should-be-aware-of-for-2024/

[xxviii] Peter G. Peterson Foundation. (2024). Why are Americans paying more for healthcare? Retrieved from https://www.pgpf.org/blog/2024/01/why-are-americans-paying-more-for-healthcare

- HealthManagement.org. (2024). Adapting the future of healthcare to an ageing population. Retrieved from https://healthmanagement.org/c/hospital/News/adapting-the-future-of-healthcare-to-an-ageing-population

[xxix] Ramsey Solutions. (n.d.). How the debt snowball method works. Retrieved from https://www.ramseysolutions.com/debt/how-the-debt-snowball-method-works

[xxx] Frontline Financial Services. (n.d.). The 70-30 rule. Retrieved from https://bit.ly/70-30Rule

[xxxi] Edmunds. (n.d.). What is the total cost of owning a car? Retrieved from https://www.edmunds.com/car-buying/what-is-the-total-cost-of-owning-a-car.html
- Consumer Reports. (n.d.). How much does it cost to own a car? Retrieved from https://www.consumerreports.org/car-insurance/how-much-does-it-cost-to-own-a-car/

[xxxii] CARFAX. (n.d.). Vehicle history report. Retrieved from https://www.carfax.com/blog/vehicle-history-report
- AutoCheck. (n.d.). Why run an AutoCheck vehicle history report? Retrieved from https://www.autocheck.com/vehiclehistory/autocheck/en/

[xxxiii] Kelley Blue Book. (n.d.). Why a pre-purchase car inspection is important. Retrieved from https://www.kbb.com/car-advice/pre-purchase-inspection/
- Edmunds. (n.d.). How to inspect a used car before buying. Retrieved from https://www.edmunds.com/car-buying/how-to-inspect-a-used-car-before-buying.html

[xxxiv] U.S. News & World Report. (n.d.). What to look for on a test drive. Retrieved from https://cars.usnews.com/cars-trucks/test-drive
- Edmunds. (n.d.). The best way to test drive a car. Retrieved from https://www.edmunds.com/car-buying/the-best-way-to-test-drive-a-car.html

[xxxv] Experian. (2022). 12 steps to take before renting your first apartment. Retrieved from https://www.experian.com/blogs/news/2022/07/12-steps-to-take-before-renting-your-first-apartment/

- Bungalow. (n.d.). Step by step guide to getting your first apartment. Retrieved from https://bungalow.com/resources/first-apartment-guide

[xxxvi] Realtor. (n.d.). Renting an apartment for the first time: A guide for new renters. Retrieved from https://www.realtor.com/advice/rent/renting-an-apartment-for-the-first-time/

- Redfin. (n.d.). 8 key tips for a first-time apartment renter. Retrieved from https://www.redfin.com/blog/first-time-apartment-renter-tips/

[xxxvii] BlackRock. (n.d.). How to invest in bonds. Retrieved from https://www.blackrock.com/us/individual/education/how-to-invest-in-bonds

[xxxviii] Bankrate. (n.d.). Stock market basics for beginners. Retrieved from https://www.bankrate.com/investing/stock-market-basics-for-beginners/

[xxxix] Forbes Advisor. (n.d.). Cryptocurrency for newcomers: A beginner's guide. Retrieved from https://www.forbes.com/advisor/investing/cryptocurrency/cryptocurrency-for-newcomers-beginners-guide/

[xl] NerdWallet. (n.d.). How to invest in mutual funds. Retrieved from https://www.nerdwallet.com/article/investing/how-to-invest-in-mutual-funds

[xli] NerdWallet. (n.d.). How to invest in ETFs (exchange-traded funds). Retrieved from https://www.nerdwallet.com/article/investing/how-to-invest-in-etf-exchange-traded-fund

[xlii] InvestmentNews. (n.d.). Investing in REITs for beginners. Retrieved from https://www.investmentnews.com/guides/investing-in-reits-for-beginners

[xliii] Mashvisor. (n.d.). House hacking a fourplex. Retrieved from https://www.mashvisor.com/blog/house-hacking-fourplex/

[xliv] Simplify101. (n.d.). How to create a vision board. Retrieved from https://simplify101.com/organizing-blog/create-vision-board/

[xlv] Erin Condren. (n.d.). Journaling goals and inspiration. Retrieved from https://www.erincondren.com/inspiration-center-journaling-goals

[xlvi] Duke Recreation & Physical Education. (n.d.). Accountability partners: Don't achieve your goals alone! Retrieved from https://recreation.duke.edu/story/accountability-partners-dont-achieve-your-goals-alone/

[xlvii] Forbes. (2023). Accountability groups: The support you need to succeed in 2023. Retrieved from https://www.forbes.com/sites/rhettpower/2023/01/05/accountability-groups-the-support-you-need-to-succeed-in-2023/

Made in the USA
Monee, IL
13 December 2024

73478034R00085